Productive Tensions

Management on the Cutting Edge series

Robert Holland, series editor
Published in cooperation with *MIT Sloan Management Review*

The AI Advantage: How to Put the Artificial Intelligence Revolution to Work
Thomas H. Davenport

The Technology Fallacy: How People are the Real Key to Digital Transformation
Gerald C. Kane, Anh Nguyen Phillips, Jonathan Copulsky, and Garth Andrus

Designed for Digital: How to Architect Your Business for Sustained Success
Jeanne W. Ross, Cynthia Beath, and Martin Mocker

See Sooner, Act Faster: How Vigilant Leaders Thrive in an Era of Digital Turbulence
George S. Day and Paul J. H. Schoemaker

Leading in the Digital World: How to Foster Creativity, Collaboration, and Inclusivity
Amit S. Mukherjee

The Ends Game: How Smart Companies Stop Selling Products and Start Delivering Value
Marco Bertini and Oded Koenigsberg

Open Strategy: Mastering Disruption from Outside the C-Suite
Christian Stadler, Julia Hautz, Kurt Matzler, and Stephan Friedrich von den Eichen

The Transformation Myth: Leading Your Organization through Uncertain Times
Gerald Kane, Rich Nanda, Anh Nguyen Phillips, and Jonathan Copulsky

Winning the Right Game: How to Disrupt, Defend, and Deliver in a Changing World
Ron Adner

The Digital Multinational: How to Connect and Compete in a (De)Globalized World
Satish Nambisan and Yadong Luo

Work without Jobs: How to Reboot Your Organization's Work Operating System
Ravin Jesuthasan and John W. Boudreau

The Future of Competitive Strategy: Unleashing the Power of Data and Digital Ecosystems
Mohan Subramaniam

Productive Tensions: How Every Leader Can Tackle Innovation's Toughest Trade-Offs
Christopher B. Bingham and Rory M. McDonald

MITSloan
Management Review

Productive Tensions

How Every Leader Can Tackle Innovation's
Toughest Trade-Offs

Christopher B. Bingham and Rory M. McDonald

The MIT Press
Cambridge, Massachusetts
London, England

The MIT Press would like to thank the anonymous peer reviewers who provided comments on drafts of this book. The generous work of academic experts is essential for establishing the authority and quality of our publications. We acknowledge with gratitude the contributions of these otherwise uncredited readers.

This book was set in Stone Serif and Stone Sans by Westchester Publishing Services. Printed and bound in the United States of America.

Library of Congress Cataloging-in-Publication Data

Names: Bingham, Christopher B., author. | McDonald, Rory M., author.
Title: Productive tensions : how every leader can tackle innovation's toughest
    trade-offs / Christopher B. Bingham and Rory M. McDonald.
Description: Cambridge, Massachusetts : The MIT Press, [2022] | Series: Management on the cutting edge | Includes bibliographical references and index.
Identifiers: LCCN 2021045980 | ISBN 9780262046930 (hardcover)
Subjects: LCSH: Leadership. | Organizational change—Management. | Conflict
    management.
Classification: LCC HD57.7 .B53434 2022 | DDC 658.4/092—dc23/eng/20211026
LC record available at https://lccn.loc.gov/2021045980

10 9 8 7 6 5 4 3 2 1

To Nellie
—CB

To Anne
—RM

Contents

Series Foreword

The world does not lack for management ideas. Thousands of researchers, practitioners, and other experts produce tens of thousands of articles, books, papers, posts, and podcasts each year. But only a scant few promise to truly move the needle on practice, and fewer still dare to reach into the future of what management will become. It is this rare breed of idea—meaningful to practice, grounded in evidence, and *built for the future*—that we seek to present in this series.

Robert Holland
Editor in chief
MIT Sloan Management Review

Introduction

This book is about fostering and leading innovation in dynamic environments—that is, in domains characterized by novelty, resource constraints, and uncertainty.

Organizations in such environments are routinely destabilized by technological change, global competition, and industry disruption. Over 90 percent of high-potential new ventures fail to reach their projected targets.[1] Few established organizations revitalize themselves enough to remain dominant over time; even fewer generate above-average shareholder returns for more than a couple of years.[2] For organizations that persist, efforts to innovate and grow can backfire. Repeated mistakes often prove enormously costly in both money and time and provide an opening for competitors. Of the tens of thousands of new products launched each year, roughly three quarters fail (and that's the hit rate of products actually *released*).[3]

What is the fundamental problem here? Do corporate CEOs and innovation teams lack the right talent? Are engineers and product designers not creative enough? Are nascent markets and new technologies too complicated and unstable to comprehend?

We think the prime explanation is that conventional approaches to leadership—the methods that many innovators use to mobilize resources, design viable business models, and launch novel products and services—are simply inadequate.

Dynamic environments require constant adaptation and transformation, but few leaders know how to navigate the tensions created by destabilizing forces. They struggle to tackle innovation's toughest trade-offs. Taking the wrong action at the wrong time is worse than doing nothing at all.[4] Successful innovation is so elusive, so hit-or-miss, that many executives settle for tweaking operational efficiency or acquiring enterprises that have proved successful.

Demystifying Leadership in Dynamic Environments

Why is innovation success so hit-or-miss? The most common explanation has to do with the attributes of leaders themselves. Wildly successful entrepreneurs—Steve Jobs, Oprah Winfrey, Jeff Bezos—clearly do possess a rare combination of intellect, determination, and such other entrepreneurial capabilities as flexibility and a high tolerance for risk. But this explanation is problematic. Indeed, recent research has challenged its fundamental premise. A Harvard Business School survey of startup founders and CEOs found no significant link between their personal attributes and the valuations of new ventures.[5] "Pretty much none of this stuff [executives' characteristics] moved the needle," reported Professor Tom Eisenmann, the study's author. And even self-evidently talented leaders have had their share of flops. Amazon Auctions, launched as a competitor to eBay, failed to gain traction; then there was the ill-fated Fire Phone. Even the indomitable Elon Musk has a substantial "failure résumé."[6] There are also the look-alikes—promising innovators anointed by the media as the next world-changers—who didn't prove up to the task, such as Kevin Rose of Digg, Adam Neumann of WeWork, and Elizabeth Holmes of Theranos. More to the point, the "great leader" explanation offers little in the way of actionable advice. What are mere mortals to do?

A second widely credited explanation is that some ventures succeed because they simply have more money, or have leaders who excel at attracting funding. It's noteworthy how often venture-backed startup teams and large-company CEOs base their strategies on this initial-resource endowment hypothesis, outspending competitors to tackle challenges. But the reality is that having lavish resources doesn't necessarily promote innovation success. In fact, a growing body of research demonstrates the opposite: that resource *constraints* foster creativity and innovation.[7]

A third, and disheartening, explanation is that sheer luck and happenstance play a more decisive role in innovation than people think. As one pundit, Nassim Nicholas Taleb, warns, we must be on guard not to be "fooled by randomness." The high failure rates of both startups and corporate innovation initiatives seem to align with the "it's all luck" explanation. So do executives' invocations of "bad timing" and laments that "the market wasn't ready" for their clever idea. Lean into luck, we are told; embrace uncertainty. Leaders are urged to take their cue from professional poker players and adopt a probabilistic approach to everyday organizational decisions by "thinking in bets."[8] Venture capitalists apply this approach when they back ten companies, hoping that lavish returns from one home-run investment will make up for nine duds. But this solution isn't feasible if you don't have multiple hands to play and don't preside over a portfolio of promising startup investments. What can you do when you're an entrepreneur or corporate innovator charged with making a single organization—your own—succeed?

A Missing Alternative Explanation

We don't subscribe to any of these popular arguments. And though at first blush, the alarming number of innovation misfires seems to argue for the "problem is too complicated to be understandable" theory, we believe the real issue is that successful leadership in dynamic environments is not well understood.

We aim in this book to expand the scope of inquiry by pinpointing and analyzing the key processes—action steps and sequences—associated with leaders' effectiveness. In an effort to understand as thoroughly as possible how organizations capture opportunities in different markets, and the ensuing patterns of success and failure, we studied nascent businesses, young companies seeking to expand, and established companies pursuing growth. We conducted hundreds of in-depth interviews at organizations on five continents (North America, South America,

Asia, Africa, and Europe) and in a diverse array of industries, including financial technology (fintech), retail, personal genomics, digital gaming, drone technology, and hospitality.

Our informants represent numerous business functions and a range of hierarchical levels, from lower-level managers to top-management team members (founders, CEOs, board chairs, executive vice presidents, corporate innovation chiefs, and business unit leaders). We interviewed both entrepreneurs and corporate innovators, as well as market analysts and financial journalists.

This research revealed something quite unexpected: the most effective leaders tend to adopt similar patterns of behavior. These patterns often defy conventional precepts about innovation and business building. In our view, they represent a powerful new body of knowledge that can help other leaders avoid both predictable and unpredictable pitfalls and chart more successful courses in dynamic environments.

Where Does Understanding Come From? From Evidence to Theory

Even something as complex as leadership in a dynamic environment can be systematized. But despite the enormous amount of evidence we compiled, evidence alone doesn't produce the coherence and direction that leaders need and want. Understanding ultimately arises from theory about what causes what, and why.

Practitioners often have little patience for theory, equating it with abstraction, impracticality, and slim reliance on data.[9] But we all rely on theories constantly; the mental models we depend on to make everyday garden-variety predictions and inferences are coherent theories about cause and effect. Will Google Maps really guide me to my destination? Leaders too make decisions and craft strategies using mental models that predict which steps taken in which sequence will lead to the outcome they envision. And in fact, leaders' failure to recognize their reliance on unexamined theories, and failure to interrogate those models, can result in using the wrong mental model at the wrong time in the wrong circumstances.

To ensure leaders understand and trust the theories advanced in this book, we followed best practices for developing new theories. We took an inductive multiple-case approach to our research: deriving new insights from comparisons of different organizations (interested readers should consult the "On Theory and Methodology" section at the end of the book for more details about this method). Such an approach is similar to the one that medical scientists, judges, physicists, and practitioners in other evidence-based professions use to reach conclusions about causality from an array of evidence. An inductive multiple-case approach equips us to build theories from carefully selected case studies, which in turn shed light on how and why particular things happen in a real-world context.[10] Each case represents its own experiment, in a sense, which can be compared and contrasted with other cases. From the patterns that emerge from analysis of multiple cases, we build propositions, develop new theories, and ultimately present a comprehensive picture of how to lead innovation effectively.

Our approach requires careful sampling of cases. In some instances, we chose polar types—cases that began similarly but followed different paths to their outcomes. For example, to develop the insights presented in chapter 2, we studied five organizations—two that performed well, two that did poorly, and one that fared OK—to build a theory about leading business model innovation in new markets. The theory in chapter 8 is built on "racing cases"—enterprises with similar starting points and similar conditions, such as founders' backgrounds and funding, that reached a shared endpoint (a fully executed strategic pivot) at different paces. Such careful case selection permitted us to isolate outcome-determining processes and behaviors. Our inductive method, in conjunction with pertinent data from prior research, also enabled us to offer prescriptive arguments. Rather than merely describing what happened, we attempt to explain why—and thus why leaders can expect the same outcomes to result from similar actions in similar situations.

The theories and lessons presented in the chapters that follow are designed to be easily understood and applied. The goal of management research ought to be to help people in organizations become better at what they do. We have approached this book with a wide variety of leaders in mind: it's for anyone charged with steering an organization's growth, innovation, and change efforts. Our ideas are thus relevant to startup teams navigating the ambiguous early stages of venture formation, to innovative employees spearheading new initiatives amid resource constraints, and to corporate executives embarking on bold strategies of reinvention.

The eight chapters that follow provide readers with a portfolio of strategies, extracted and generalized from the lived experience of innovation leaders in a range of industries, settings, and types of enterprises. Some of these strategies call for self-scrutiny, in the sense of rigorously examining one's own assumptions, habits of mind, and thought processes. They are built, in part, on the marketplace experiences of able predecessors who have gotten it right and then gotten it wrong. There is much to be learned from the experiences of those who, despite experience, passion, shrewdness, dedication, and good ideas, have fallen prey to pitfalls and missteps.

Getting It Right Matters, Getting It Wrong Happens

Consider Henri Seydoux, a French inventor in the drone industry whose idiosyncratic leadership contributed to his company's uneven trajectory. In 2010 Seydoux's company, Parrot, introduced the AR Drone—a smartphone-controlled quadcopter (one with four rotors) that was ahead of its time. Seydoux had been quick to recognize the vast array of follow-on possibilities that accompanied the advent of smartphones. Seeking to combine the thrill of flying drones with the fun of video games, Seydoux innovated around three phone features—music, photography, and games.[11] The Parrot AR Drone launched at the Consumer Electronics Show in Las Vegas. People were immediately intrigued. The product was the show's main attraction and the subject of nearly three hundred TV reports.[12]

But pitching a product that lacked business precedent to established retailers proved more problematic. "Retailers didn't know where the products should sit. Toys? Phone peripherals? Hobby? We tried numerous categories and positioning, in our efforts to actually create a category well ahead of it actually existing," Parrot's chief sales and marketing officer later reported.

Meanwhile, another group of drone innovators, DJI Technology, realized that adding an action camera to a drone would open up an array of possibilities. Within two years, DJI had won about 70 percent of the commercial market worldwide and as much as 85 percent of the consumer market. Experts reported that the DJI drone's photographic quality was unmatched. It quickly became known as "the flying camera." By 2019, Parrot, hemorrhaging cash, was forced to exit the consumer market.

How did a pioneering innovative company become an also-ran in the industry it helped create? Its leaders struggled with an array of tensions. Sales and marketing executives weren't sure how to frame their innovation to maximize adoption (should they stress a drone's similarity to retailers' existing offerings or emphasize its novelty?). Innovation teams, wary of reliance on data for markets that didn't yet exist—hence the prohibition on market research—nonetheless had to field requests from a board accustomed to data-driven decisions. And strategists couldn't keep track of shifting customer needs within an evolving competitive landscape. Seydoux later lamented: "I made a risky mistake. In comparison [to DJI], my drone was just a toy. The video was streamed on the user's phone, but it wasn't possible to record it. The quality was horrible. Sony and Nintendo had told me that I shouldn't sell the product for more than €300, while, in fact, people were ready to pay way more for a quality camera. We were wrongly obsessed with making the drone as cheap as possible. We constrained ourselves because the market was unknown at the time." These dilemmas all embodied tensions natural to innovative markets. For Seydoux and other Parrot leaders, the tensions of innovation proved overwhelming.

Consider another category innovator, Kevin Plank, founder of the sports apparel company Under Armour.[13] While playing college football, Plank began experimenting with fabrics that would remain dry beneath layers of evaporation-stifling protective gear[14] and ultimately discovered that polyester, which repels water, could be modified to draw moisture away from the skin and then release it (a property called "wicking").[15] Adding spandex fiber caused it to cling tightly to the wearer's body and compress the muscles, a feature believed to improve endurance.[16] Plank produced a prototype base layer, a lightweight, form-fitting, sweat-wicking, stretchy compression shirt. As the benefits of comfort and enhanced performance became clear, more and more athletes gave it a try. Twenty years of growth unprecedented in the industry followed; Under Armour surpassed $5 billion in sales by 2017. Under Armour successfully broke into the athletic apparel and footwear market—a market dominated by Nike and Adidas. How? In building the business, Under Armour's leaders effectively tackled the tensions of innovation. But they've lost that effectiveness in recent years. High-profile moves into data/wearables and fashion seem more like me-too brand extensions, placing Under Armour in head-on competition. Even as the company strayed from its original brand purpose, its revenue barely budged, and the stock price plummeted. Moreover, the Under Armour brand is increasingly out of step with consumer tastes.

For leaders in established organizations (which Under Armour had become), the tensions of innovation may be particularly daunting. Rapid changes in customer behavior and the insatiable demand for new offerings can turn core capabilities into liabilities. What gives a company its competitive advantage changes over time, and so leaders too must change the way they operate. (Under Armour's Plank, who had weathered several calls for leadership change, stepped down in 2019.)

The Structure of the Book

Each chapter of this book is designed to help leaders succeed at managing tensions in dynamic environments. The tensions inherent in innovation are enduring inconsistencies that arise from competing aims: efficiency or flexibility? consistency or change? product or purpose? They provoke anxiety, consume leaders' time, and require solutions. The conundrum is that leaders are often unable either to identify these tensions or to navigate their way through them competently.

The chapters spotlight eight critical tensions that every innovator must master. How do you excite customers about a product they've never imagined? When is it wise to accept what the data are telling you, and when should you ignore the data and plow forward anyway? How can you retain stakeholders' trust and support during radical unforeseen course corrections? Many leaders regard such tensions as impossible trade-offs, and reluctantly force themselves to choose between narrowly conceived paths. Readers will learn that outcomes tend to be much better when leaders view tensions as productive, and will gain ample practical guidance on harnessing tensions effectively. We guide you through innovation's thorniest tensions, using examples drawn from the experience of organizations as varied as P&G, Instagram, the US military, Honda, In-N-Out Burger, Slack, Under Armour, and the snowboarding company Burton.

The following chart specifies the tensions and the related questions we address in this book, by chapter.

Chapter	Title	Tension	Question
1	The Opportunity Paradox	*Selection vs. execution*	How can we capture new growth opportunities most effectively?
2	Parallel Play	*Differentiation vs. borrowing*	How can we determine which points of differentiation will be most important to would-be customers?
3	Defer to or Ignore the Data?	*Accept vs. ignore*	When should we defer to data and when should we ignore data?
4	Crowd Sequencing	*Inside vs. outside*	How can we best leverage the knowledge of others, both within and outside the organization?
5	Rational Heuristics	*Efficiency vs. flexibility*	How can we avoid reinventing the wheel but remain open to reinvention?
6	Framing Innovations Effectively	*Familiar vs. novel*	How can we frame innovations to garner resources, attention, and traction?
7	Product versus Purpose	*Product vs. purpose*	How can we create a unique brand advantage and sustain it over time?
8	When It's Time to Pivot, What's Your Story?	*Consistency vs. change*	How can we maintain trust and project a consistent vision during inevitable adaptation?

Chapter 1, "The Opportunity Paradox," introduces the tension between the optimal ways of selecting opportunities and executing them. Some leaders, and even some scholars, argue for following the money and letting opportunity choice be tied to emergent customer demand, not to a preset plan. This opportunistic approach has both intuitive and rational appeal in settings characterized by a swift and unpredictable flow of opportunities, shifting market boundaries, and ever-changing competitors. Does this mean that a disciplined approach is for losers? Far from it. Our research generated a clear roadmap for when to remain disciplined and focused and when to be receptive and opportunistic. Disciplined planning during opportunity selection early on may even pave the way for more latitude in opportunity selection later.

Chapter 2, "Parallel Play," explores the tension that leaders face between competitive differentiation and borrowing. Brand-new markets are like wormholes in science fiction, where the usual laws of time and space are suspended: when a market has just come into being, the forces of competition are constantly in flux. Since it's unclear who your customers will be, conventional strategies don't make sense. How should you navigate this constantly shifting terrain? We discovered that the most successful leaders in dynamic environments engage in a practice known as "parallel play," observing their surroundings and their peers' activities and testing out their ideas, just as preschoolers do. They also borrow ideas unapologetically. Only after relentless experimentation do they commit to a single template for creating value. Even then, rather than quickly optimizing, they leave that template partially undetermined and pause, watch, and wait. As they accumulate insights, and as the market begins to settle down, they refine their model bit by bit.

Chapter 3, "Defer to or Ignore the Data?," takes a hard look at how to use data in decision-making. We live in a golden age of data analytics: new capabilities driven by data analytics promise to turbocharge companies' disruptive potential, a prospect whose plausibility is attested to by the data-driven ascendancy of Facebook, Amazon, Netflix, and Google. But pathbreaking innovations are inherently contrarian, and evaluating them requires nuance and interpretation, not simply deferring to data. How should innovation-seeking leaders engage with data? We look to great scientists as exemplars: like great leaders, outstanding scientists forge new paths by exploring promising ideas, unsupported by data, that eventually transform the paradigms of their respective fields. Their work strongly suggests that the pursuit of breakthroughs requires an approach to data that is fundamentally more skeptical than deferential.

Leaders who operate singlehandedly are subject to information-processing limits; their information is incomplete, and what they know is inevitably distorted by cognitive bias. Left uncorrected, these shortcomings can result in poor outcomes. In chapter 4, "Crowd Sequencing," we detail how leaders need to reach out for help, both inside and outside the organization, to drive change and innovation. Using crowds—that is, the groups of people around us—to generate and refine solutions is an effective way to overcome the inherent limitations of individual cognitive processing, particularly in dynamic environments where leaders must make rapid decisions in unpredictable situations. How can leaders best tap the potential power of crowds? The answer lies in a new strategic phenomenon we call *crowd sequencing*. In essence, it entails activating different crowds at different times to address different types of uncertainty. This approach can increase the odds that leaders solve the right problems, know whether they've found the right solutions, and pinpoint the right resources and skills to execute solutions.

Most organizations tend to add more structure over time. They create policies and playbooks that promote bureaucracy and inertia. Chapter 5, "Rational Heuristics," spotlights a counterintuitive insight: when environments become more complex, the best strategies often take the form of simple rules of thumb, or heuristics. Many observers scorn heuristics as knee-jerk substitutes for analysis and invoke them to explain irrational behavior and strategic failure. The purpose of this chapter is to shed light on how carefully crafted heuristics can help organizations; we spell out what types of heuristics leaders should create, and why. We also outline how leaders can ensure that their rules of thumb don't generate their own bureaucracies over time.

Chapter 6, "Framing Innovations Effectively," outlines the tension between familiarity and novelty when innovations are to be introduced. As the pace of innovation increases, human perception more than technological benefit is likely to govern whether new products and services are adopted or rejected. If leaders fail to emphasize what's familiar, audiences won't feel comfortable enough to give the innovation a chance. But downplaying novelty can suppress the attraction and curiosity necessary to drive trial and adoption. When to stress familiarity and when to stress novelty are essential questions in any organization attempting to innovate. Our research suggests that initially, an innovation should be introduced by stressing its similarities to an existing product or service. Later, growing familiarity allows accentuating the novel. We offer strategies for getting the successive framings right, and for effectively managing the transition between framings.

Chapter 7, "Product versus Purpose," explores the tension between product and purpose. Building a successful brand is every marketer's dream. Well-designed "purpose brands" can sell themselves, command premium pricing, and lock out competitors. But far more new brands fail than succeed. Why? Largely because leaders focus too single-mindedly on a brand's identity and image when they should be perfecting its purpose, which is to help customers do a particular job. We offer a three-step approach to integrating branding and marketing with product development: (1) identify how a product or service can meet customers' functional, emotional, and social needs, (2) ensure that customers' experiences while purchasing and using the product do the job faultlessly, and (3) develop and align processes to make the brand synonymous with the job to be done. Once a purpose brand gains traction, it's time to figure out whether to take yet another step, using the purpose brand to endorse and legitimize other products.

Finally, chapter 8, "When It's Time to Pivot, What's Your Story?," delves into the tension between consistency and change. Newly formed ventures and initiatives typically deploy compelling narratives about their offerings to rally investors, staff, customers, and the media. But often that narrative turns out later to be strategically wrong, requiring a change of direction.

How that shift is communicated to stakeholders can have a huge impact on a venture's future. Our research identifies a set of stratagems for maintaining stakeholder support during pivots. Early on, leaders should avoid communicating specific solutions in favor of issuing a compelling, visionary, but nonspecific rallying cry. Then, if a course correction is necessary, they can signal continuity by explaining how the new plan accords with the original vision. Once the reboot has taken place, it's essential to be conciliatory and empathetic toward stakeholders, who may feel abandoned or betrayed. Employees and customers are far more apt to remain loyal if forewarned about how they'll be affected and if leaders communicate genuine caring.

Overall, the different chapters spotlight innovation's toughest tensions and the central questions they embody. Using lots of examples from a range of diverse industries, we also offer practical and novel solutions to effectively manage each tension. Leaders will improve their odds of success not by persistently tackling one tension but by developing the ability to tackle different tensions at different times as the context requires. While challenging, this outcome is achievable with concerted effort.

The path to becoming a better leader has always been, and will continue to be, long and rocky. It takes both tenacity and time to traverse it. But the rewards are often monumental. Our aspiration is to help all leaders on that journey by providing cutting-edge, evidence-based tools to better navigate the changing nature of their industries and environments. By shedding needed light on how tensions can be productive, we hope that the practices and processes discussed in this book will become integral to leading innovation.

I Charting a Course

1 The Opportunity Paradox: How Can Organizations Capture New Opportunities Most Effectively?

Flexibility or discipline? Which stance positions leaders best to capture new growth opportunities? Both the question and the answer, it turns out, are more complex and nuanced than was previously understood. Our research on new ventures, growing businesses, and mature corporations found an ongoing tension between flexibility and focus that can define or break your business. This chapter explores when to be focused and disciplined and when to be flexible and opportunistic.

Many leaders assert that growth should be planned. Planning helps leaders chart a course for the achievement of goals, develop "what if" scenarios, identify risk factors, and prepare for contingencies in a more comprehensive way. This approach is consistent with research findings that performance often benefits from adhering to standardized templates for new-market entry.[1]

But some practitioners and scholars argue that planning rarely succeeds in dynamic environments. They endorse extensive experimentation, adaptation, and improvisation.[2] This approach has both intuitive and rational appeal in an uncertain world where the flow of opportunities is swift and unpredictable, market boundaries are ever-shifting, and the competition is constantly changing.[3]

In a competitive environment that calls for change and flexibility, is a strategic emphasis on careful planning obsolete? We argue that it isn't. In fact, our interviews with a wide array of leaders revealed that treating the two stances as mutually exclusive is a mistake—and, counterintuitively, that focus may even enhance a company's flexibility, and vice versa.

Opportunities are complex. To begin with, every opportunity has two parts: *opportunity selection* and *opportunity execution*. Opportunity selection involves deciding which customer problem to solve; opportunity execution entails solving that problem.[4] Most publications and most thought leaders focus heavily on execution, on creating value by developing a solution for customers. But research suggests that innovators often rush to execution so hastily that they must backtrack later on to figure out exactly what problem they are trying to solve.[5] In other words, opportunity selection appears to matter as much as opportunity execution, the arena in which companies tend to spend the most time. More important, how you approach opportunity selection—with flexibility or with focus—can have a decisive impact on how successful you will be at execution.

Opportunists versus Strategists

Our research revealed that leaders of innovation tend to cluster in one or the other of two groups that we call *opportunists* and *strategists*.[6] Organizations, too, tend to be either opportunistic or strategic. Opportunists rely on a less scripted, more flexible approach to opportunity selection. Instead of mapping out ahead of time the types of opportunities they will pursue, opportunists let customer inquiries shape opportunity selection. For example, a US-based security software company chose to enter the German market because a German customer had expressed interest in its security monitoring services. The same company's decision to enter Switzerland was a response to unforeseen customer demand there, not a deliberate plan to do so. "It was more like we were drawn in," an executive later remarked about that decision, "rather than a conscious decision."

Opportunists view themselves as astutely cherry-picking low-hanging fruit, or seizing narrow windows of opportunity before they close or competitors capture them. Rather than developing detailed plans that might prove flawed or outdated or both, they take advantage of what emerges. This flexible approach to opportunity selection is consistent with the strategy and entrepreneurship literature, which argues that the dynamic nature of many markets lessens the value of pre-action deliberation and, further, that ambiguity is not necessarily undesirable. Indeed, many business leaders make better decisions on the fly than as the outcome of focused planning.[7]

Strategists, by contrast, having watched companies that pursue emerging opportunities lose focus by trying to address the needs of multiple markets, choose to limit themselves to particular markets to channel their efforts toward the opportunities most likely to succeed. As a result, strategists are more disciplined. They begin by studying the nature of opportunity capture in their market. Then they devise a plan to focus on what they consider the best (not just the easiest) opportunity that would allow them to capture several follow-on opportunities in succession, rather than just one.

For example, a Finland-based company that helps firms manage inventory by point-of-sale software selected its first foreign market, Sweden, based on how much its leaders could learn there—not just on their ability to make a sale. Though not a large market, Sweden was both culturally similar and geographically nearby. This scenario reduced the risk that the company's leaders would be overwhelmed by cultural differences and increased the likelihood that they could learn how to do business there. As the CEO explained, "We were quite conservative in this process, because we didn't know much about international business. So we started with Sweden." After Sweden, the company chose Norway, then France, Germany, and the UK, and later the US. It thus gained experience in progressively larger markets and exploited its growing knowledge. In general, focused opportunity selection allows companies to pursue easier or more foundational opportunities first; those opportunities in turn set the stage for more difficult or less foundational opportunities. Sequencing is key when building a bridge or assembling a computer; it also appears to be critical to effective opportunity capture.

Flexible Selection and Inflexible Execution

How do these divergent patterns of opportunity selection unfold? We were surprised to find opportunists, who are more flexible in the selection phase, to be less flexible in the opportunity-execution phase. In other words, these managers are adept at responding on the fly to emerging opportunities, but once they begin to execute, many become surprisingly rigid. At a US-based medical imaging software company, for example, leaders were very flexible about the selection of opportunities. "We were trying to get something going in Europe," one cofounder noted, "so we looked for opportunities and we cherry-picked." The company decided to enter Sweden on the strength of interest in its software expressed by some doctors there. But after the company had entered Sweden, they and other doctors appeared reluctant to substitute a new technology for an established method of mammography.

The company, instead of flexibly changing its solutions to meet local market preferences, continued trying to sell a universal product. Its executives selected their second country, Norway, in the same ad hoc fashion; when sales there didn't materialize, the company's leaders declared that the targeted customers didn't understand the product. Rather than adjusting their approach, they pushed existing solutions. This pattern—flexibility in opportunity selection but rigidity in opportunity execution—often leads to poor results. Commenting on their entry into Sweden, executives at the medical imaging company remarked: "We could not sell into Sweden" and "Our sales people ran off a cliff. They went nowhere." Performance in subsequent countries was similar.

Focused Selection and Flexible Execution

Conversely, and equally surprisingly, organizations that are more disciplined and rigid about opportunity selection tend to be more flexible at opportunity execution. The founders of a Singapore-based gaming company thought long and hard about which markets to enter. On the strength of customer interviews and market observations, management concluded that the best way to tackle multiple markets was to begin with Japan. But selling digital content to Japanese wireless providers required going head-to-head with Japanese content providers, who were technically competent and entrenched in the market.

In response, management stopped trying to sell original content in Japan in favor of selling their Japanese competitors' content throughout Asia. "Instead of competing with them [Japanese content companies]," the

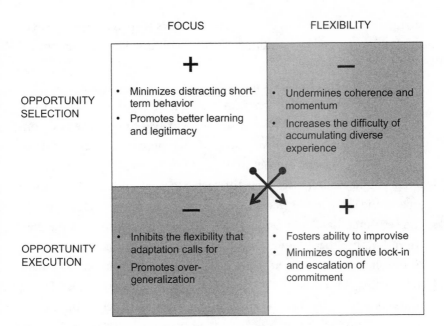

Figure 1.1

chairman explained, "we decided to partner with them and take their products and sell them throughout Asia." The outcome of executing flexibly in Japan was greater success than the original plan would have generated. "Once we decided to partner with [Japanese companies to sell their content], within three months we [had] signed up quite a lot of very reputable content makers," one company executive reported. We observed a similar pattern at other companies: increased discipline in opportunity selection results in increased flexibility in opportunity execution (see figure 1.1).

Lessons on Opportunity Capture

Our research thus produced two provocative mirror-image observations about opportunity capture that are fundamental to achieving growth in new markets: (1) opportunists can be remarkably flexible about selecting opportunities but tend to be considerably more rigid about executing them, and (2) strategists can be painstakingly rigorous about selecting opportunities but typically are more flexible about executing them. These patterns can be traced to the ways we perceive ourselves as careful decision-makers and how we deal with unfavorable outcomes.

The Perils of Cognitive Lock-In

Our research suggests that opportunistic leaders are prone to what we call *postdecision cognitive lock-in*, or a strong tendency to embrace and continue to reiterate positive perceptions of their opportunity choices. They tend to rely on several distinct strategies to do so. We observed that they often rationalized choices after the fact, focusing only on the positive aspects and ignoring the negatives. In a similar vein, they tended to blame choices' undesirable outcomes on external circumstances beyond their control, rather than questioning how rashly they had made the choice in the first place. Thus the potentially corrective impact of discordant information was minimal. Finally, reluctant to give up or change a failing course of action, they often doubled down, increasing their commitment.

For example, executives at a Finland-based security software company selected the company's opportunities flexibly (unlike the Finnish point-of-sale software company described above, which selected its opportunities in a much more disciplined manner). Entry into its first foreign market, Sweden, was not planned in advance. As the chief financial officer admitted, "Sweden was very much ad hoc." Later, however, managers claimed that Sweden had been deliberately selected as a location where employees could "cut their teeth." When sales in Sweden fell short, company leaders began blaming external factors, such as their customers' financial positions, rather than faulty strategy. As a result, they did not alter their method of executing opportunities. A senior leader explained that the company had worked hard to develop a standard template for providing services: "We just would not budge on that," he said. These restrictive policies prevented the company from working out agreements with several prospective customers when it attempted to enter the United States.

Such rationalizations sometimes function as a sense-making device for executives. That is, rationalization often goes hand in hand with a face-saving shift of attention to aspects of an opportunity that they had

ignored during the opportunity selection phase.[8] Such a shift of attention can fend off unease about dimensions of the opportunity that were
taken into account but are proving disappointing or problematic.[9] This
pattern reveals a paradoxical observation about opportunity capture: the
more leaders attempt to control opportunity execution, the less control
they are likely to be able to achieve. This lack of control stems largely
from trying to standardize solutions for users and situations that are
inherently unique. Interestingly enough, longer executive experience
seems to further discourage flexible execution at opportunistic companies. This pattern suggests that prior successes at executing opportunities
may tend to become institutionalized in organization practices.

Strategists, by contrast, systematically appraise only a few opportunities within the broader array of possibilities. This orderly process of
opportunity selection results in less need to justify faulty choices after
the fact, and thus allows leaders to approach execution more open-
mindedly. As a result, they tend to adapt and experiment, sometimes
opting for radical changes to their product or business model. One
company we studied, a provider of IT security software, carefully studied its opportunity set and chose China as the best market to enter.
To management's surprise, several Chinese customers were reluctant to
pay for software—they were accustomed to free software bundled with
purchases of hardware. The team thus switched gears and developed a
hardware solution, which sold very well.

Generally speaking, we found, strategists are more likely than opportunists to modify their opportunity execution: they are better able to
abandon existing products and practices and to adopt more appropriate new ones.

The Benefits of Sequencing Opportunities

Another fundamental insight is that long-term growth in new markets
depends on sequencing opportunities for learning. At first glance, flexible opportunity selection would seem to encourage managers to learn
and adapt. We found, however, that many of the most flexible managers and entrepreneurs had come face to face with a couple of important

lessons. First, it's difficult to learn if you are constantly changing course. Second, sustained business success appears to depend less on capturing a single golden opportunity than on stringing multiple opportunities together. Hence longer-term success hinges in part on understanding how capturing one opportunity can prepare managers and organizations to capture others.

Creating a sequence for opportunity capture enables leaders to link the present to the future in a way that promises to facilitate team alignment and channel the energies and attention of geographically dispersed employees and managers. This process helps an organization to adopt a rhythm and move forward in a synchronized fashion. Sequencing thus calls for an orderly approach to opportunity selection—assessing where the organization is now, where it wants to go, and the path to get there—that serves as an alternative to using emerging customer demand to select opportunities.

Because opportunists often select the opportunity that looks as if it can be brought to fruition fastest, they frequently find it difficult to learn from and build on their efforts. Managers of established businesses often expressed skepticism that the various opportunities they were chasing had anything in common; they were also often dubious about the lessons learned. Managers of newer businesses complained that chasing multiple markets suggested a lack of vision. Both sets of executives had a surfeit of data—on customer needs, feedback, and product features—that pulled them in multiple directions. As a result, it was hard to know what to do to succeed. For instance, the CEO of the Finnish security software developer discussed earlier acknowledged his team's difficulties applying the lessons they had learned: "We should have had more focus and more country-by-country-specific plans, rather than just trying to cover all the bases in a shotgun approach." Similarly, a US entrepreneur we interviewed recalled ruefully, "We were doing so many things that it wasn't clear what we were learning from any of it. Every time we made a change, we changed so many things [that] it wasn't clear what caused what."

By contrast, strategists—who by definition are more disciplined about opportunity selection—tend to be attentive to sequencing the opportunities they have chosen. They often select markets based on the ability to learn from them and to prepare for the next one. For example, an entrepreneurial US developer of learning tools decided to focus on delivering quizzes to the education market. Asked why, he explained: "By focusing on a single problem for a single market, we could actually really start to learn what solved customers' problems. We began to really understand what educators needed, and what would lead to more revenue." By narrowing his focus, the entrepreneur was able to increase revenue 400 percent the following year. He then applied what he had learned from educational testing to move into testing for business enterprises, where he found even greater success.

Another example of leaders acting as strategists is the snowboarding company Burton. Deliberately sequencing opportunities enabled the company to transform a backyard hobby into a thriving global business and an Olympic sport. Jake Burton Carpenter, who founded Burton in 1977, was obsessive about making top-quality snowboards; he created one hundred prototypes before producing the Burton Backhill, one of the world's first commercial snowboards. "I learned the hard way that you cannot presume anything is going to work well. You have to think through every possible failure and test the hell out of products," Carpenter said. "When you are out there in the freezing cold and something breaks, it is a real letdown. Our mantra is to assume the product will fail—and then make sure it does not."[10] After creating superior wooden snowboards for backcountry use, he leveraged his knowledge to move on to the next opportunity: superior snowboards for use at ski resorts. The addition of a P-tex (polyethylene) base, clip-in boot bindings, and metal edges for use on hardpack groomed runs brought Burton both revenue and recognition.

The next opportunity was to expand the product portfolio; Carpenter added racing boards to the lineup. As a user-entrepreneur, he spent more than one hundred days a year on the hill, where he absorbed fellow boarders' complaints about both unreliable boards and unreliable equipment, such as flimsy boots, gloves that ripped easily, and pants and jackets that didn't stand up to the wear and tear of snowboarding. Burton then leveraged its expertise in hard goods (boards and bindings) to enter soft goods (boots and clothing), where profit margins are even higher. Carpenter described the sequential nature of opportunity selection: "We started out with snowboards. But then it became clear that people needed specific footwear for them. So we got into boots. And then we started making jackets, and then more technical waterproof outerwear. I pushed product extension. There were naysayers and purists who would say, 'We can't make long underwear!' I'd counter, 'Yeah, we can!'" Over time, Burton strategically sequenced opportunities in a way that entrenched the brand and made it increasingly popular. Doing so helped Burton be able to sponsor the best professional riders (three-time Olympic gold medalist Shaun White and three-time medalist Kelly Clark) and to command 35 percent of the $350 billion snowboard equipment market.

In addition to pursuing learning systematically, strategists also sequence opportunities to enhance their legitimacy and credibility in the marketplace. For example, a Singapore-based provider of semiconductor solutions for wireless devices aspired to sell in the US market but recognized that it needed to establish a track record first. To do so, it began selling to customers in Taiwan, leveraged those sales to win business in Korea, and eventually lined up customers in the United States, Germany, and Japan.

Similarly, the running shoe brand Hoka One One (pronounced "o-nay o-nay") also owes its meteoric rise to sequenced selection of opportunities to build legitimacy. At the time of Hoka's launch in 2009, minimalist running shoes dominated both mainstream and specialty stores. Hoka wanted to move in the opposite direction, toward "maximalism," or maximally cushioned running shoes. Founders Nicolas Mermoud and Jean-Luc Diard began by creating a slip-on overshoe for rugged mountain races in the Alps, Pyrenees, and Dolomites. They then created a conventional running shoe and began promoting it at specialty races and boutique running shops. Meanwhile they pursued legitimacy and credibility by sponsoring two of the world's top trail runners, Dave Mackey and Karl Meltzer. Only then did Hoka enter the mainstream marketplace. Its shoes can now be found at hundreds of retail shops and in races around the globe; the company enjoys consistent double-digit sales growth. Depending on circumstances, sequencing can also proceed in reverse, from the high end to the broader market: Tesla Motors decided that selling high-end electric vehicles would promote electric vehicles in other segments of the market.

Overall, the benefits of sequencing are easy for leaders to comprehend, but the implementation entails considerable cognitive sophistication: it takes time to acquire insight into how opportunities can and should be ordered. This may be one reason why sequencing appears to be employed more frequently by older companies and companies whose founders have more experience.

How to Select Opportunities

Resist Easy Opportunities

A few guidelines can help rationalize opportunity selection. To begin with, resist jumping at easy opportunities. Restraint may be hard to come by when cash is limited and the new opportunity appears to exploit the company's existing capabilities. An example of lack of restraint is one of Uber's first nonridesharing initiatives, the now defunct service UberRush. Riding high on its success with ridesharing, Uber believed itself capable of taking on logistics giants like FedEx, Amazon, JB Hunt, and Ryder. Using its existing app and resources, the company moved rapidly from introducing a network of bike delivery dispatchers to providing delivery for retailers. As CEO Travis Kalanick told *Vanity Fair*, "If we can get you a car in five minutes, we can get you anything in five minutes."[11] By the time it launched, the company had signed up such big names in retail as Shopify, Nordstrom, Dick's Sporting Goods, Harris Teeter Supermarkets, and Delivery .com. The goal was to deliver such goods as pizzas, shoes, flowers, athletic equipment, and clothing to consumers soon after they placed orders.

At first glance, UberRush appeared to call for resources and capabilities similar to those of Uber's ride-hailing service, including many of the same drivers. Had Uber been more thorough in its assessment of the opportunity, however, its leaders would have recognized decisive differences between the new businesses. For instance, Uber could have foreseen that few people need daily delivery services as urgently as they need transportation. And its leaders could also have seen that the service UberRush offered—delivery by bike messengers and private vehicles—wasn't a good fit for many organizations' delivery needs. As one former employee commented, "If you want to move stuff in a city, you're basically talking about flowers and dry cleaning." In other words, transporting larger loads, such as catered food and furniture, isn't feasible with a Toyota Prius. Thus the opportunity was actually quite remote from Uber's existing strengths, which entailed providing predictable services that the company could thoroughly control. UberRush, by contrast, called for design and implementation of a unique delivery network for one-off use, in which organizational partners would want greater control. After spending eighteen months on the effort, which the company had boldly claimed would transform the logistics industry, Uber shuttered UberRush. The lasting lesson for Uber leaders? Don't jump at easy opportunities without fully thinking them through.

Take the Long View
Leaders should ask themselves, What does the right opportunity look like, and how will it position us for future opportunities? Remember the lessons on sequencing: look for how opportunities might link together in a sequence. Will one opportunity position you for another? Will the first opportunity help you to learn about the next? Will it confer the legitimacy to capture future customers?

The founders of the Singapore-based digital gaming company discussed earlier applied these criteria when they assessed opportunities to build their consumer business in Asia. In their case, the sequence identified was to begin in Japan and then move on to Taiwan and Hong Kong before going after other markets. One founder remarked, "The digital content business is really a consumer business. And looking at Asia's development for consumer business—whether it's fashion, or electronics, or whatever—the trend always starts in Japan, and progressively moves to Taiwan and then to Hong Kong, and then to the rest of the market. I mean, this trend has been like that for the last fifty years. So when we pushed consumer-based, consumer-oriented digital products, that's the same thing we did. We started by securing supplier ships from

Japan and pushed to the next most obvious market, which is Taiwan. Once consumer products were accepted in Taiwan, then we progressed even more to other markets."

Consider All the Options, Not Just Immediate Ones

Think about your full array of choices, taking into account such criteria as the opportunity's size (Is it large enough to be worth your time?), its reachability (Does the company have or can it develop capabilities to capture the market?), and the competition (How crowded is the field of competitors?). Many managers make the mistake of chasing opportunities that are too small to be worth the time or big opportunities that are out of reach or too competitive. Nasdaq illustrates the latter. It entered the energy futures space in 2015, largely in response to pleas from Goldman Sachs, JPMorgan Chase, Morgan Stanley, and others to innovate around energy trading. Those firms argued that Nasdaq could cut the cost of trading the world's biggest energy futures contracts by up to 50 percent. Convinced by their arguments, and excited about the opportunity, Nasdaq's chief executive, Bob Greifeld, inaugurated the business, known as NFX. Its overarching aim was to break into energy markets dominated by the US rivals CME Group and Intercontinental Exchange (ICE). CME and ICE closed ranks, aggressively fighting Nasdaq for market share. Existing traders were already locked in to other marketplaces and, because of Nasdaq's inexperience in the energy space, unwilling to switch to NFX. The not-so-surprising outcome for Nasdaq was an expensive exit from the business.

Behaving like a strategist rather than an opportunist may be particularly important for younger businesses. By considering each opportunity's unique characteristics and how they link to other opportunities, entrepreneurial companies can more readily overcome inherent liabilities of newness (e.g., lack of resources and lack of a track record),[12] accumulating experience in a manner that builds on the past while enhancing credibility. That is how Dropbox built credibility with the enterprise market.[13] The company's founders, recognizing that the enterprise market would be difficult to break into because of its complex decision-making processes and numerous gatekeepers, focused on the lower-barrier personal file storage market to build initial traction and credibility. "The idea is to get people using it inside companies without IT's permission," explained Drew Houston, one of Dropbox's founders. "Once IT sees that Dropbox is in heavy demand and that it works reliably, we'll get certified for use across the company. This approach worked for Wi-Fi equipment and Blackberrys. That's been our go-to-market strategy for enterprise: personal use as a Trojan horse."

How to Execute Opportunities

Once you select an opportunity that is apt to link to further opportunities, remember that execution requires a flexible, rapid, and iterative learning cycle. Though choosing similar products and establishing consistent practices is important to capture efficiencies, our research shows that continued emphasis on routine actions can hobble companies' ability to adapt and to walk away from losing situations.

Leaders should begin by designing a series of experiments to test what customers want, and then rapidly adjust offerings to meet their needs. Many of the companies we studied made radical changes to their products and business models—changes as extreme as shifting from software to hardware or from providing content to reselling it—on entering a new market. Some of the most successful strategists walked away from apparently attractive opportunities after their initial experiments because they experienced less regret than opportunists. Strategist leaders knew they had thoughtfully selected the best opportunity from a broader set of possibilities and thus were more willing to adapt during execution.

In most cases, successful execution depended on (1) regular interaction with customers and (2) openness to adapting in response to negative results, rather than assigning blame or firing the sales team. For example, one Singapore firm aimed to help customers manage information security risks. The founders designed a sequence for country entry based on which countries were viewed as most attractive at different stages in the foreign market entry process. One said, "When I started the company I immediately started in Singapore and Hong

Kong because from those two countries you can cover North and South Asia." The founders explicitly intended to expand gradually into countries like Malaysia and China based on the firm's two locations. When the firm entered Malaysia, the country manager sought to promote the firm's core 24×7 security monitoring service. He soon realized, however, that growth was flat owing to Malaysia's relatively weak technology backbone compared to that of Singapore or Hong Kong. Although Malaysian customers believed in the importance of 24×7 security monitoring, they first needed basic security infrastructure. Executives thus decided to abandon their security monitoring product and focus instead on creating new infrastructure products. One said, "Malaysia is still developing, and there is a lot of security infrastructure that was not set up. Either firewall or intrusion detection systems (IDS) is not set up, i.e., there is nothing for us to monitor. It gives us a lot of opportunities to actually go in to do things like security system integration. That is where we help them to set up an infrastructure like firewall and IDS."

The Opportunity Audit

What if you have been too opportunistic about selecting opportunities and too rigid about executing them? And how can you tell whether your way of selecting and executing opportunities needs improvement? We recommend an opportunity audit, built around the following questions:

- How did you choose the opportunities you are currently chasing?
- If you could start over, which opportunities would you choose? Which opportunities lend themselves best to building a rational and powerful sequence?
- What are the results of your current efforts? What are common explanations of poor performance? What might be done to help avoid making excuses?
- If the company were threatened with bankruptcy today, which single opportunity would you keep? Which opportunities would you give up?

After answering these questions, don't be afraid to make radical changes. Throwing good money after bad is a common trap; people tend to intensify their commitment to a failure they feel responsible for. A more rational choice is to let it go and adopt a more disciplined process to opportunity selection. Counterintuitive as it may seem, this approach will foster the flexibility you will need for opportunity execution.

Conclusion

Few recognize that opportunity capture is a two-phase process, consisting of opportunity selection and opportunity execution. Intensified focus and discipline during opportunity selection, achieved through sequencing, can promote flexibility during opportunity execution. By contrast, lack of discipline during selection can constrain learning and adaptation (see table 1.1). Moving from focus to flexibility during opportunity capture equips organizations to reap the benefits of concentration while leaving room for change.

Table 1.1
Managing the opportunity paradox

Instead of doing this . . .	Do this . . .	And get this result . . .
Thinking broadly about opportunity capture	Realize that opportunities have two phases: opportunity selection and opportunity execution.	More specificity and thoughtfulness in strategic decision-making
Acting flexibly during opportunity selection	Be more focused during opportunity selection.	More flexibility in execution of opportunities
Selecting opportunities in response to emerging unanticipated customer demand	Be disciplined about analyzing opportunities and the linkages among them.	Improved learning; increased legitimacy and credibility over time
Chasing small opportunities that don't merit the time, big opportunities beyond your reach, or middle-sized opportunities that are too competitive	Think about your full array of choices, taking into account opportunity size (Is it large enough to be worth your time?), reachability (Can the company capture the market?), and competition (How crowded is the field of competitors?).	Portfolio coherence, which enhances performance by promoting coordinated activity and cumulative learning

2 Parallel Play: Why the Usual Rules of Competition and Strategy Don't Apply in Emerging Industries and Product Categories

The past two decades have witnessed the birth of an unprecedented number of new-to-the-world markets. Technologies such as cloud services, warehouse robotics, and smartphones have redefined entire industries, making old business categories obsolete. A steady stream of still emerging innovations—from commercial drones and autonomous trucks to virtual and augmented reality to plant-based meat substitutes—suggests that the era of market creation will continue for the foreseeable future.

In new markets, the questions that typically define an organization's strategy—where to play and how to win—have no easy answers. Large organizations with lavish budgets may find themselves outflanked by brash startups; today's winners may be tomorrow's losers. PayPal, for example, is now the clear leader in online payments, but in that market's early years the top competitor was a company called Billpoint. 23andMe took an early lead in personal genomics, but it remains to be seen which firm will ultimately dominate that market.

It's tempting to think of pioneers in new markets as entering a totally unfamiliar terrain without recognizable landmarks or proven navigational tools. But our research into patterns of success and failure in new markets has uncovered something unexpected.

Over the past few years, we've conducted hundreds of interviews with entrepreneurs and corporate innovators in fields ranging from personal genomics and augmented reality to drones and technology-enabled finance (fintech).[1] What we've learned is that the most successful of these pioneers follow the same set of implicit rules and share specific behaviors. These rules and patterns often defy conventional precepts of strategy and business building. In our eyes, they add up to a new strategic framework—one that can help other innovators chart a course in new markets and avoid the pitfalls they present. This chapter delves into innovators' business models and tackles a vexing tension between *differentiation,* or seeking uniqueness to distinguish oneself from a competitor, and *borrowing,* or knowingly using or imitating other organizations' ideas. We outline how savvy leaders navigate what to copy and from whom as they make their way to an innovative business model.

An Alternative to Conventional Strategy

In traditional business thinking, the essence of strategy is choosing to perform activities differently from the way rivals do. A winning strategy positions an organization to deliver some sort of value better than anyone else does: to serve a particular set of customers more effectively, for instance, or to provide greater benefit at lower cost, whatever the source of the intended advantage may be. The job of the strategist is to identify competitors—existing and potential—and then to outmaneuver them. Venture capitalists reinforce this mindset by requiring founders of startups to list their competitors and to explain how they plan to distinguish themselves from the pack.

In a new market, however, this approach makes little sense. When a market (or a business category) is still forming, leaders can't possibly know which points of distinctiveness are likely to matter most to customers. Moreover, the competition typically consists of small ventures that are equally in the dark. Conventional strategy frameworks just don't apply. An analysis of the five forces that, in Michael Porter's classic formulation, affect a competitive environment—existing rivals, the bargaining power of suppliers and of customers, alternative offerings, and new entrants—is apt to be less productive when those forces are in constant flux and may suddenly emerge or disappear. (Porter has acknowledged as much: in a new industry, he has written, "managers face a high level of uncertainty about the needs of customers, the products and services that will prove to be the most desired, and the best configuration of activities and technologies to deliver them.")[2]

By definition, established companies have established business models. They know how to create value in a given space, and the primary strategic question is how to do so in a way that allows them to outstrip the competition. By contrast, companies in a new market don't know what business model will actually make sense; most can't even answer the age-old questions "Who is the customer?," "What does the customer value?," and "How will we deliver that value at an appropriate cost?" They may have hypotheses, but they cannot know whether their hypotheses will pan out. Consider the early days of the ride-sharing business. In early 2012, Uber offered black cars operated by drivers with commercial licenses and charged premium prices. Zimride was a carpool-matching service for universities and companies. A company called Sidecar was seeking to become a multipassenger, multistop ride service featuring drivers with ordinary licenses. None of those fledgling business models survived intact.

The uncertainty of new markets requires a different framework for strategic thinking. We call it "parallel play."[3] Its inspiration comes from an unlikely setting, early childhood. As child psychologists have long known, three- and four-year-olds typically behave in a distinct fashion in a social setting: they play near one another but not together. They keep an eye on what their peers are doing (and sometimes copy them) but soon revert to their own projects—building a block structure, say, or creating a costume from old clothes. Occasionally they'll grab a toy from another child. The more precocious among them may pause periodically to assess what they've done and then continue on a slightly different tack. Though aware of other children's efforts, they focus primarily on their own activities and on figuring out what works as they progress toward whatever goal they have in mind.

We asked executives operating in new markets to describe the strategic steps they had taken as their companies and industries evolved. We identified patterns in those descriptions and then compared the patterns with the corresponding companies' progress. That's when we discovered that the behavior of successful new-market pioneers bears a striking resemblance to that of preschoolers. They learn about their markets and their customers—and about what is likely to work—in much the same way that young children move around their world.

How Parallel Play Sets Organizations Apart

Parallel play is a natural way to behave when you don't know very much. Three kinds of parallel play behaviors in particular distinguish high-performing new-market companies from their less successful rivals.

1. Early on, forget about differentiation. Borrow ideas instead. When young children playing side by side observe one another, each one learns more than he or she could have by playing alone. Preschoolers often imitate one another and borrow others' toys, but rarely do they bother trying to outdo each other. Borrowing is also typical of successful new-market innovators. Again, the ride-sharing category offers a good example. Sidecar opted to reduce the complexity inherent in its multipassenger, multistop model by substituting one-passenger, one-stop rides.[4] The drivers would use their own cars, and the system would offer such in-app features as electronic payments, GPS navigation, and a rating system for drivers. Suddenly, those methods of creating value made the most sense to everybody. Zimride's service emulated Sidecar closely; the company eventually changed its name to Lyft. Uber was not far behind, creating what it then called UberX to distinguish the peer-to-peer service from its corporate black car service.

Astute borrowing can make the difference between a winner and an also-ran. In 1999 Google founders Larry Page and Sergey Brin knew they had created a search engine superior to anything else available at the time. What they didn't know was how to make money with it. Display ads were out of the question—Page and Brin considered them ugly, and they took too long to load. But the company was hemorrhaging cash. The two founders looked around and decided to borrow an idea from GoTo.com, a rival search engine that was generating ample revenue by allowing advertisers to pay for prominent placement in search results—but charging them only when users clicked on their ads.[5] Google's new product, AdWords, introduced in 2000, maintained the integrity of search but let advertisers buy small text ads that would appear above the results. Like GoTo, Google charged only for clicks, not for views.

The practice of borrowing contradicts the conventional strategic imperative of differentiation—which traditional strategists argue is essential to avoid the negative spiral of competing only on cost. But trying to differentiate early on in a new market can lead an organization down a blind alley. A more effective approach, we argue, is to treat other companies in the space as peers rather than competitors. When we interviewed executives in a nascent fintech category, we learned that one firm was so focused on distinguishing itself that it spent millions developing a slick user interface and proprietary algorithms to scrape data directly from brokerage accounts, nearly going broke in the process. Meanwhile, a successful rival pursued a different approach: it reproduced a peer's user interface (rather than spending resources to develop its own) and opted for a financial analytics provider that other fintech companies had already hired to gain access to shared brokerage data. Borrowing enabled the company to develop a working prototype of its product quickly and cheaply.

To be sure, borrowing is unlikely to produce an optimal business model, which is the foundational task of a new enterprise. Treating peers as a treasure trove of ideas and resources from which an organization can draw won't identify the product that all customers will value over existing solutions, or the best mechanism to profitably deliver it. But borrowing typically shrinks the amount of money and time needed to design a good-enough-for-now offering. By minimizing direct trial-and-error learning, secondhand learning reduces the number and severity of hard lessons and allows leaders to concentrate more fully on other aspects of the business model and on testing assumptions. Borrowing also helps leaders resist the temptation to strive for an optimal solution right away—an unrealistic and unnecessary aim in a brand-new market. At this very early stage, quickly assembling a rough prototype for purposes of hands-on learning is nearly always a more useful aim than pursuing a perfect solution is.

Of course, leaders may borrow faulty ideas. But as long as they focus on how to profitably deliver value to customers, they're likely to be reasonably astute judges of whether a given idea is sound. And if multiple peers are all doing the same thing—as in the case of the fintech companies all working with the same financial data broker—there's probably a good reason.

This is not to say that leaders in new markets shouldn't differentiate. But initially, we argue, their primary competitive focus should almost always be on an existing substitute—what the customer currently uses—rather than their new-market rivals. Ride-sharing companies came to view themselves as competition for the taxi industry, and ultimately for private car ownership. Google's objective was to supplant conventional advertising. The successful fintech companies we studied viewed established investment and wealth management firms as their true competition. In their messages to prospective customers and investors, they all presented themselves as superior to traditional sources of financial guidance. They mostly ignored their fintech peers (preferring to "play the course, not the players," as one company founder memorably expressed it).

An early focus on established substitutes helps leaders create a realistic value proposition. At a stage when peer-company "competitors" are likely to have few users, established substitutes are already providing value to customers. As one fintech founder put it, viewing established substitutes as the real rivals prevented his team from "worrying about the wrong things." To be sure, this focus can be hard to achieve in practice; many venture capitalists demand benchmarks against other startups, but enlightened investors and founders find other ways to measure progress. "At the early stage we are looking for companies that are *non-consensus*—[that] have a unique insight that defies conventional wisdom—not companies that are better than competitors," says Ann Miura-Ko, a partner at Floodgate, a seed stage venture capital firm that has backed Twitter, Lyft, and Cruise Automation. "The point isn't to fit in to someone else's landscape or category."

2. Test relentlessly—and then commit. When young children play, they tend to explore various projects and then turn to the one that engages them most. The idea of developing innovations through experimentation and testing is by now widely accepted,[6] though many companies continue to make the mistake of launching without much testing. But in a new market, we discovered, high-performing ventures didn't just test and learn from market feedback. They used that learning to choose a single template for creating and capturing value (i.e., for monetization) and spent their scarce resources only on it.

This approach goes against conventional strategic teaching that, in uncertain markets, the cost of commitment and the ensuing loss of flexibility can't be justified. But our research revealed commitment to be key to success—provided that firms tested alternative business model templates first. Less successful enterprises either committed without testing (often missing out on more lucrative opportunities) or flitted among several templates, hedging their bets without making a choice.

When the app Burbn—which enabled users located near one another to connect, arrange to meet, and post photos of their meetups—proved too complicated, discouraging use of most of its features, founder Kevin Systrom began running tests to discover a template that captured what users really wanted.[7] The outcome was a business model centered on photo sharing. Systrom doubled down on making it possible to post a good photo with three clicks, and scrapped everything else.[8] He then renamed the app Instagram. Later, Systrom unapologetically borrowed the "stories" feature from Snapchat and incorporated it into Instagram. ("They deserve all the credit," he acknowledged to a reporter.)

Evernote offers a cautionary counterexample. Having begun as an elegant note-taking app, Evernote tried to morph into a lifestyle brand in response to strong interest from investors. The company built a chat app, a recipe app, a contact management app, and a flashcard app, while embracing two very dissimilar business model paths: apps built on a freemium model (a basic product offered for free, to entice users to pay for a higher-end version) and online sales of goods.[9] Although Evernote lives on, it failed to live up to expectations. It started with a strong, useful concept, but the organization's lack of commitment to a single template for creating and capturing value derailed it.

For new-market enterprises, the choice of a template is a decisive fork in the road. Look at the experiences of PayPal and its erstwhile rivals in the nascent digital payments sector. Both eMoneyMail and Billpoint forged close relationships with established banks, with the aim of combating fraud. Both also limited their markets: after less than a year of operation, eMoneyMail made its service available only to Bank One customers.[10] Similarly, eBay, which had acquired Billpoint, discouraged use of the service outside its own auction site. Executives at both companies regarded a close banking relationship and a limited customer base as necessary to win consumers' trust and to keep fraud expense within manageable limits. Meanwhile, PayPal's leaders took a different road. They committed to an open, stand-alone, web-based model available to all, and learned from testing that ease of use was more critical to users than tight antifraud controls. Thus, as *Wired* reported, the organization's leaders came to view fraud as "something akin to an R&D expense." PayPal "reimbursed customers for their losses, learned how the crooks worked, and engineered ingenious fixes" such as the now familiar "type this" codes presented in a GIF file.[11] Commitment to its business model encouraged PayPal to innovate in ways that its rivals on another path never gave a thought to.

3. Pause, watch, and refine. Preschoolers' parallel play frequently involves making things, such as a sand castle or a doll's costume. As we noted earlier, some children take a break periodically to reflect on their projects before continuing. We observed similar behavior on the part of high-performing innovators in new markets: after committing to a general approach to creating and capturing value, they paused and looked around before nailing down the specifics of that business model.

This step may be the most striking of our challenges to conventional theories of strategy, nearly all of which assume that commitment and a full-speed-ahead pace are the same thing. At classic lean startups, entrepreneurs and corporate innovators aim to identify potential customers, pinpoint what those customers value, and aggressively optimize their

operations to deliver it in a profitable way.[12] If something goes awry, the
theory is, the venture can quickly pivot to a new business model ("fail
fast"). But in an evolving market, trying too early to perfect a business
model, even one that appears to be working well, can be problematic.
And pivoting can be costly, difficult, and time-consuming since it typically involves unwinding and rebuilding aspects of the business model.
(Chapter 8 discusses stratagems for managing the pivoting process more
effectively.) It's often preferable, we learned, to leave a business model
purposely undetermined. Leaders at the most successful companies initially specify the basic elements of their business models (e.g., a product that some customers will find superior to existing solutions and the
resources to deliver it) but leave other elements undefined (e.g., a full set
of product features and mechanisms for delivering it to various customer
groups). In other words, they commit to a single template for creating
and capturing value but postpone optimizing it. Figure 2.1 summarizes
the three kinds of parallel play behaviors discussed here for organizations.

Dropbox's early history offers insight into the benefits of watchful
waiting. The startup created enormous value by giving customers instant
access to their files from any computer through a simple drag-and-drop
interface; early on, it committed to an easy-to-use product and a freemium model for capturing some of that value.[13] Interestingly, though, the

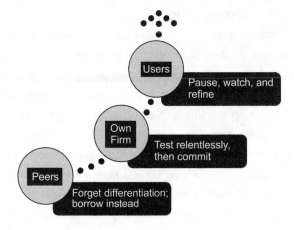

Figure 2.1

venture stopped short of tailoring its offering to consumers (though they were Dropbox's primary users at the time) or building operations around the original and most salient use case (backing up files). With its robust but undetermined model, Dropbox was able to accommodate additional use cases—sharing files and collaboration—and profitable new customers: enterprises. By the time it filed to go public, in 2018, about 30 percent of its 11 million paying users were on a Dropbox Business team plan.[14]

Any new market is likely to present surprises—unforeseen customers and uses that no amount of testing would have revealed. An incomplete, partially elaborated business model increases the likelihood that innovators will be able to accommodate useful new information that they could not have anticipated. As one fintech investor explained, "The fewer constraints we impose, the better, because there's more room for emergent behavior, more room to discover." A purposely undetermined business model also allows leaders' activities to evolve in step with a changing market. In nascent markets, users' preferences shift as they engage with innovations in unexpected ways. For example, the portable ultrasound pioneer SonoSite created a website where health care providers could share how they used its ultrasonic stethoscope. The website helped Sono-Site learn about unintended uses and customers, such as nurses locating a vein before inserting a needle and medical missionaries diagnosing heart defects in children.[15] These discoveries enabled SonoSite to refine its business model accordingly.

The new-market graveyard is filled with companies trapped by their original business models. Take Shyp, which aimed to pick up and ship consumers' packages for as little as $5 (plus postage). For a while the company grew fast, reaching a $250 million valuation; then growth slowed and losses caught up with it. Instead of pausing to explore other potential sources of value, such as shipping for businesses, founder Kevin Gibbon and his team kept rushing onward.[16] Shyp ended up shutting down in early 2018. Companies whose leaders take a breather before refining their models, in contrast, learn by waiting and observing—an approach that is more likely to produce unanticipated insights than are other types of learning. Because pausing is inexpensive, it is relatively low risk. Leaders can readily resume refining the business model when the team is no longer learning much or when peers appear to be sprinting ahead. The activity that is on hold during a pause relates to business model design. Normal day-to-day operations—including, potentially, marketing—continue during a pause.

Consider the experience of Rent the Runway (RtR), a venture in the brand-new market for stylish rental clothing. Founders Jenn Hyman and Jenny Fleiss initially envisioned a "closet in the cloud" from which women could rent designer clothes for occasions like weddings. They tested the idea by inviting 140 women to two pop-up events. These tests helped them profile potential customers and provided insight into peripheral questions, such as whether renting clothing was an activity that women would pursue alone or together.[17]

Though the initial business gained popularity, the company wanted to expand its range of offerings. A subscription-based offering of accessories and handbags met with lukewarm success. The founders then turned to watchful waiting; they also looked closely at how their customers hoped to use RtR. Most customers, they realized, spent five days a week at an office. They didn't just want special occasion clothing; they also wanted stylish apparel for work.[18] When RtR expanded in that direction, its growth was assured. Companies in mature markets have long turned to customers and the insights they provide to drive innovation[19]; new-market companies can too.

It makes sense to ask why committing to a business model template is effective in new markets but fully executing it immediately is not. Investing in two or more distinct models is simply too confusing and too costly. But once the commitment to a single one has been made, leaders can moderate the pace at which they refine elements of the model and gather serendipitous insights through passive learning.

Conclusion

The precepts of new-market strategy do not mean that the conventional rules of strategy should be abandoned. After a few years—the interval varies considerably, depending on the industry—a few companies will become standouts in each new market. They are likely to reap the usual benefits that strategists identified long ago: network effects, economies of scale, market power, and so on. Rent the Runway now operates in an increasingly crowded market—both startups and established retailers are dipping their toes into subscription clothing services—and might need to leave its parallel play approach behind. Startups inevitably grow up, and the markets they pioneered become established industries; at that point they must begin to observe the traditional laws of strategy and focus on competition. Every organization that hopes to succeed over the long term will eventually need one or more sources of differentiation.

Leaders innovating in new markets resemble children in that there is much they don't yet know. They operate in utterly strange but fascinating environments, where discovery and surprise are a constant. It makes perfect sense, then, that the most successful of them behave like preschoolers, engaging in parallel play and borrowing, testing, and looking around to see what happens (see table 2.1).

Table 2.1
How to parallel play your way to an innovative business model

Instead of doing this . . .	Do this . . .	And get this result . . .
Differentiating from competitors early on in a new market	Borrow ideas from peers, and make established substitutes your main competitive focus.	Creation of a realistic value proposition since early-stage competitors are apt to have few users while established substitutes already provide value to customers
Hedging bets by adopting several business model templates	Test alternative business model templates quickly and relentlessly, then commit to one.	Less confusion, better focus, and improved allocation of scarce resources
Trying to perfect a business model—even one that appears to be working well—too early	Pause, watch, and refine while leaving your business model purposely underdetermined.	Acquisition of information that you could not have anticipated; evolution of your activities in step with a changing market

II Navigating the Path

3 Defer to or Ignore the Data? How Setting Aside Data (Selectively) Can Enable Pathbreaking Innovations

Netflix's success is often attributed to its clever use of data analytics. The company's vertically integrated platform provides its managers a revealing window into the viewing habits of more than 180 million customers. They know what people are watching and for how long. They know when users pause or rewind episodes; they know how long it takes viewers to watch an entire series. They track customers' ratings, searches, and browsing behavior.[1] They also meticulously analyze movies' content and tag them with metadata denoting their levels of gore, romance, humor, and plot conclusiveness, and even the characters' moral status.[2] These metadata, matched with data on customers' viewing habits (and with Netflix's vaunted algorithm, which offers recommendations based on user preferences), are widely believed to give the company a distinct advantage when competing for potential blockbusters. It's also allegedly why the company's first original release, *House of Cards*—a $100 million bet on self-produced content—was such a big success. It wasn't *guessing* that customers would enjoy a political thriller set in Washington, D.C., and awash in money, sex, and power. Netflix *knew* they would.

A more intriguing but less widely known story is how *Stranger Things* was approved for purchase when the data predicted it would flop. Netflix's data showed very clearly that programs featuring kids didn't fare well; neither did '80s nostalgia, or shows featuring Winona Ryder. But *Stranger Things* was greenlighted and went on to become Netflix's most binged show ever.

How did this happen? The answer is that Netflix's public image as a data-driven organization is misleading: it doesn't accurately capture the role of data in the innovation process. Yes, data analysis is central to the company's decision-making, along with projection models and cost analyses, but it is far from the sole consideration, especially when it comes to evaluating the potential of truly novel projects. Netflix's chief content officer, Ted Sarandos, explains: "Data either reinforces your worst notion or it just supports what you want to do, either way."[3] If executives feel passionate enough about a new project, Sarandos says, they sometimes ignore the data completely—a surprising admission from the organization widely viewed as the epitome of data-driven decision-making.

The Preeminence of Data Analytics

We live in the golden age of data analytics. Digital platforms, wireless sensors, apps, and mobile phones all amass huge quantities of data, whose volume doubles every few years.[4] Computing power is increasing fast; the costs of capturing, storing, and processing data are falling. The prevailing orthodoxy that data analytics promises to unlock companies' disruptive potential is reinforced by the fact that the tech behemoths Facebook, Amazon, Netflix, and Google are all highly data-driven.

In this environment, managers are preoccupied with generating data to describe their terrain in ever-increasing detail. No sooner does a business launch than it begins to generate data on sales, costs, customers, operations, products, competitors, engagement, and clicks. When internally generated data aren't enough, managers buy data sets from a growing pool of aggregators, whose business model is built on buying and selling unstructured or semistructured data collected through passive surveillance of people navigating the web, as well as trade reports that summarize and extrapolate from prevailing trends.[5] These data sets are accompanied by simplified models that implicitly claim to predict the future with certainty.

Such data—tangible and readily communicable—are widely treated as the foundation on which leaders ought to ground their decisions about the future. Want to know what product to develop, or how to price it, or how much money to invest in it? Check the data. Many managers consider data the most objective and trustworthy justification for a path forward. This strategy can pay off, of course. But when it comes to taking huge leaps—creating a pathbreaking innovation, say—a fundamentally different approach is called for. Not only can data be insufficient, they can get in the way. This is the case because pathbreaking innovation is inherently contrarian. "You have to be very cautious not to get caught in the math, because you'll end up making the same thing over and over again," says Sarandos. "And the data just tells you what happened in the past. It doesn't tell you anything that will happen in the future."[6]

Sarandos doesn't mean that data are always a poor predictor of the future. (Data forecast incremental advances in stable environments quite accurately.) His point is that pathbreaking innovations have the potential to make clean breaks from the past. Data, even data about causal relationships, can describe the past accurately but should not impose constraints on what might be possible in the future. The data were absolutely correct that viewers disliked shows about kids in the '80s—that is, until *Stranger Things* came along and made the '80s cool again.

Evaluating potential pathbreaking innovations requires a more nuanced approach than simply deferring to data. How, then, should leaders seeking such innovations engage with data? This chapter looks to great scientists as exemplars: like great innovators, great scientists advance progress and forge new paths. Such scientists champion controversial ideas that eventually transform the paradigms of their respective fields. Their work demonstrates that, in science as in innovation, breakthroughs require an approach to data that is fundamentally more skeptical than the deferential posture that currently prevails in organizations.

Why Some Scientists Ignore Disconfirming Data

Several years ago, the sociologist Eric Leifer spelled out the scientific case for ignoring data in "Denying the Data: Learning from the Accomplished Sciences."[7] Leifer took his fellow sociologists to task for their "passive" approach to data, by which he meant accepting data without recognizing and questioning data's inherent limitations. Here's what happens: when data do not support a theory, instead of questioning whether the data are appropriate for evaluating the theory, many social scientists conclude that the theory is false. They defer to the data: "You can't argue with the data." These social scientists genuinely believe that the data disprove the theory, and are making a good faith effort to get closer to the truth. The end result is that data are allowed to disqualify potentially useful theories.

Great scientists like Galileo and Einstein, Leifer pointed out, were unconcerned with explaining existing observations; their aim was to create effects or objects that had never before observed. In some cases these scientists went further: they clung to their theories, ignoring data and even laboratory results that didn't align with them.

In mature scientific fields such as physics, scientists begin with a theory and aren't easily swayed by disconfirming data. When it comes to big breakthrough ideas, physicists may ignore data completely. Einstein, for example, had a vision of how the world works, which led to his theory of relativity. His famous "thought experiments"—imagined consequences of physical interactions without any supporting data—told him that light was affected by gravity. At the time, no data supported this theory; what limited data there were suggested that light didn't affect gravity. Instead of working from existing data, Einstein simply ignored it. It took decades of engineering advances to create experimental conditions capable of producing the data that supported Einstein's theory. Galileo, a similarly avid user of thought experiments, apparently had even less interest in data from actual experiments. He reportedly confessed to not performing certain experiments attributed to him: "I do not need it, as without any experience I can affirm that it is so."[8]

In *The Structure of Scientific Revolutions* (1970),[9] the philosopher of science Thomas Kuhn asserted that new ways of viewing the world—new paradigms—do not result from deferring to data. The reverse is generally true, in that science does not advance by a process of accretion but rather moves forward from paradigm to paradigm. For example, Einstein didn't simply refine the existing Newtonian equations that described the attraction of objects according to their masses. He developed an entirely new way of thinking about the universe, using the curvature of space-time to explain gravity. Such shifts, because they overthrow the very foundations of the process of scientific thought, are revolutionary. Once scientists like Einstein or Galileo had formulated new theory, data to support it began to emerge.

Innovations in business seem to result from a process similar to revolutions in science. When Steve Jobs introduced the Macintosh computer, he leaned on his theory of technology, not numbers. (In the early 1980s, there were no data suggesting overwhelming unmet demand for cute desktop computers.) Jobs persisted in the same kind of ignore-the-data thinking when he introduced the iPad. He didn't care what people *said* they wanted; he sought to create something never before seen—a product that people couldn't yet imagine but would want once they saw it. "A lot of times, people don't know what they want until you show it to them," he told *Business Week*.[10]

It bears repeating that our goal is not to discredit data analytics or to call into question empirical observation in general; advances in data analytics clearly have the power to transform companies, industries, and society in significant ways. Nor are we arguing that leaders should always (or even often) ignore the data. Accepting what the data reveal makes sense in most cases, such as for improving operations, for pricing, and even for evaluating incremental innovations. But for new-to-the-world innovations and for fundamentally pathbreaking or disruptive ideas, relying on extensive data is less useful. Stunning advances typically begin with a big beautiful theory; the data to support it arrive later.

Our aim in this chapter is to encourage mindfulness about data and its uses, particularly when it comes to a reliance on data constraining or enabling certain types of innovations. We elaborate on what it means to ignore data and when it makes sense to do so. Following this advice can help leaders think and act like Einstein and Jobs by looking beyond "what is" to focus on "what is possible."

Ignoring the Data

What does it mean to ignore the data? It means to choose not to act in alignment with what data are telling you to do, to intentionally put the data aside and go in another direction. And why? Because, as Leifer explains, "The physical and social worlds are hopeless tangles of friction, accident, and failure." Simple theories cannot possibly be expected to align with such uneven, erratic, and disorganized environments.

Consider the leaves that fall from a tree in autumn. Some drop to the ground; others swirl in the air or are carried away horizontally. Someone ignorant of the theory of gravity might attribute these diverse trajectories to innate differences in the leaves themselves. Treating the leaves' trajectories as data might lead you to overlook the main story, gravity.[11]

By the same token, using the indiscriminate averaging of a random sample isn't necessarily the best way to arrive at truth. If you wanted to learn how to dance well, you wouldn't average the moves of a group of couples on a Saturday night, some perfectly in sync, others stepping on each other's feet. It might be more effective to turn your back on the dancers, put aside the data their movements generate, and picture in your mind's eye the fluidity and symmetry required to dance well.[12] Thus we can ignore much of what is observable to find something more fundamental that works better.

Just as great scientists don't necessarily abandon good theories because the data do not corroborate them, great leaders of innovation shouldn't expect clever, novel, and pathbreaking ideas to align with the data streaming from an erratic and disorganized world. Breakthroughs in business rarely fit the available data; impactful innovations won't readily align with what the A/B tests tell you. The more unconventional or contrarian the innovation, the more a manager must be willing to ignore the data along the way.

The scientists and scholars whose work has helped us most profoundly to comprehend the mechanisms behind observed phenomena have relied on establishing what they know and reasoning their way to more encompassing hypotheses that *could* be true. In the process, they have ignored certain data, and actively created conditions in which to confirm the soundness of their theories and to carry out further inquiry. Leaders of innovation within organizations may have to find the resolve to act similarly. "The spark of invention becomes what the data does not say. No amount of data can ever confirm or corroborate, since it has yet to exist," write Viktor Mayer-Schönberger and Kenneth Cukier in their foundational book, *Big Data: A Revolution That Will Transform How We Live, Work, and Think*.[13]

The Trouble with Numbers

Great leaders of innovation, like great scientists, don't cede decision-making to data; they actively engage with the data. Not only can passively deferring to data make good theories appear faulty, the data itself can be faulty. There are at least two reasons why this is the case. First, there's an infinite amount of data, and which data you choose to pay attention to will bias results. Someone has to decide what to collect and how to organize it, present it, and infer meaning from it. Second, data are, by definition, dated. Data describe the past, not the future[14]—and therefore are less revealing about what *could be*. No data are infallible, yet data fallibility is often overlooked in pursuit of quantitative order.

Some organizations create sophisticated data strategies only to realize that, like Leifer's fellow sociologists, they are using data to justify interpretations or decisions more sweeping than the data support. In the early 2000s, P&G, in an effort to make better data-driven product decisions, relied heavily on a metric it called weighted purchase intent (WPI). The WPI aggregated several hundred consumers' stated intent to purchase a pilot product after using it for two weeks. If the WPI of a new product was statistically superior to that of existing products in the market, it was approved. Because this approach was objective, managerial consensus was easy to achieve. But it also stifled innovation. Using the threshold of statistical significance erased the difference between a four-point win and a twenty-point win. Managers would run WPI tests with large samples to achieve statistical significance, thus justifying the release of products that performed only marginally better than the status quo. What's more, consumer testing became an exercise in "checking the box"; managers relied on the handy metrics and neglected to dig deeper to find out why customers liked or disliked a product in the first place.[15] And some very promising products without statistically significant results didn't get the green light. That's what almost happened to Tide Pods, one of P&G's biggest recent breakthroughs. Fortunately, despite weak internal indicators, a few senior leaders believed in Tide Pods and pushed the product through to commercialization. Partially in response to its runaway success, P&G replaced passive deference to data with a more holistic, active approach to product evaluation.

When should leaders push back against reliance on data in innovation decisions? More specifically, under what circumstances does ignoring the data makes sense? We can offer two insights (see figure 3.1):

1. When a leader aims to introduce a new-to-the-world product category

When asked whether data analytics had helped Nest design its smart thermostats, CEO Tony Fadell said no. He acknowledged that data provide unparalleled insight into the unexpected ways that customers use products, enabling organizations to improve them and build loyalty. But "great products come from strong points of view," he told *Forbes*.[16] "You design them for yourself. You say no to most of the features that data says you'll need." Fadell added that he had learned product design from helping Steve Jobs launch the iPod.

Similarly, when the French company Parrot pioneered the new-to-the-world consumer drone, its CEO, Henri Seydoux, imposed two prohibitions: no adherence to technical standards or requirements and no market research.[17] What captivates consumers today may not continue

NO   YES

Ignore Data

- When you want to meet the needs of your best (existing) customers

- When you want to overcome common financial hurdles for accepting projects (ROE, ROA, IRR, Payback)

- When you want to introduce a new-to-the-world product category and go after customers who aren't being served at all

- When disruption is afoot and your organization hopes to stave it off

Figure 3.1

often initially produce lower profit margins than do the organization's main business operations. Without erecting a barrier between the innovation process and the data used in business operations, leaders might use data to evaluate the innovation as they do their established markets, in the expectation that the innovation will contribute significantly to corporate growth or organizational renewal. When the innovation does not contribute at that level, leaders will transfer key employees from innovation projects to more profitable mainstream business operations, leaving the innovation to wither on the vine.

Netflix has taken steps to insulate its content creators from operational data. Many observers have pointed out that Netflix hides its viewing numbers from the public—but the company also keeps those numbers from most of the people involved in making shows. Netflix executives have, at times, resisted the temptation to leverage all that the organization knows about its subscribers (and their viewing habits) to guide the creative direction of its shows. "I ask for [the data] and never get it," said the creator of one hit series. "I'm always, like, 'Who do people like? You guys [Netflix] know everything! You know when someone re-watches a segment of a show, where people turn things on or turn them off.' It would be really interesting for me to know."[21] But savvy innovation managers at Netflix have concluded that it may *not* be good for creative talent to know.

Rather than requiring every decision to be backed by quantitative evidence, leaders can foster an organizational culture in which other methods—logic, intuition, qualitative insight—are also seen as legitimate. If data have already become gospel, another way to nurture potentially pathbreaking ideas is to appoint a data skeptic (or accept a volunteer) or heretic. President Kennedy embraced a similar logic when he assigned his brother Robert to play devil's advocate during the Cuban missile crisis. The data heretic's job is to hold data at arm's length if he or she feels strongly that an important contrarian idea needs to be nurtured and protected. (The data heretic may need to be deeply familiar with the data to understand their shortcomings and limitations.)

Ultimately, the best path forward often turns out to be triangulation of multiple perspectives. This is what P&G put in place after the near rejection of Tide Pods. The organization discarded its "objective metric" and embraced a more holistic approach to approving breakthrough products. "Instead of a 'check-the-box' with one number, you're going to create a body of evidence that's everything you learned on your product," explained a senior R&D officer. "And that requires a combination of art and science."[22] Marshaling multiple perspectives improves the accuracy and thoroughness of the information used in decision-making about innovation.

In summary, how leaders engage with data is consequential: it constrains or enables different types of innovation. Relying on extensive data analytics will help propel incremental innovation but will also tend to discourage pathbreaking innovation. Introducing new-to-the-world innovations and fundamentally disruptive ideas requires an approach that embraces the wisdom of ignoring, instead of deferring to, the data (see table 3.1).

Table 3.1
How active engagement with data enables pathbreaking innovation

Instead of doing this . . .	Do this . . .	And get this result . . .
Insisting on market research in a market that does not exist	Maintain healthy skepticism about insights derived from data.	Ideas that don't conform to old ways of thinking and working
Assigning decisions about existing operations and future innovations to the same people	Create a data barrier to isolate the innovation/creative process from the data used in business operations.	Protection of potentially disruptive products and pathbreaking innovations
Requiring every decision to be backed by quantitative evidence	Draw on a variety of perspectives and multiple methods (e.g., logic, intuition, qualitative insight).	Fresh insights, needed for new-to-the world innovation
Deferring to data to serve the needs of your organization's best customers	Ignore the data and think about how to go after customers who aren't being served at all.	Avoidance of disruption
Letting data become gospel	Appoint a data skeptic.	Protection and nurture of the development of new ideas and a culture of innovation

4 Crowd Sequencing: How to Accelerate Innovation and Address Uncertainty

One summer afternoon on a Florida beach, two young brothers get into trouble: they're a hundred yards from shore and a riptide is pulling them out to sea. Their mother and others hear their screams. Two would-be rescuers swim out to them but encounter the same current. Relatives of the boys follow, and soon nine people are being dragged ever farther from shore. There are no lifeguards, and no ropes in sight. A police rescue boat is on its way, but twenty minutes have passed, and some of the swimmers' heads are slipping underwater. This is the situation when Derek and Jessica Simmons arrive to find dozens of people watching helplessly from the beach. The couple tells everyone to link arms. At their direction, the group forms an eighty-person human chain that stretches out into the sea toward the swimmers. Derek and Jessica are at the front of the chain. They take turns swimming out to those in distress and hauling them back to the chain, where they are passed back person-to-person to the safety of the beach.[1]

As swimmers struggled to survive, a group watched helplessly from shore. Then two new arrivals turned up and devised a solution, one that entailed using the crowd as a tool.

The use of crowds as a tool is as relevant to organizational innovation as it is to survival in a riptide. Innovators need others' help. Alone, individuals are subject to information-processing limitations. Their information is incomplete, and what they know is affected by cognitive bias. Left unaddressed, these shortcomings can result in poor outcomes for individuals, teams, and organizations.[2] Using crowds—or the people around us—to generate solutions is an effective way to overcome the inherent limitations of individual cognitive processing, particularly in entrepreneurial settings where leaders must make swift decisions in the face of uncertainty.

How can leaders best tap the potential power of crowds? The answer lies in a novel strategic framework we call *crowd sequencing*. Crowd sequencing consists of using an assortment of crowds, or groups, to address different types of uncertainty related to innovation at different times. Effective crowd sequencing involves three steps:

1. Using crowds to ensure that you're solving the right problems;

2. Using crowds to test whether you've found the right solutions; and

3. Using crowds to execute solutions.

Using Crowds to Ensure That You're Solving the Right Problems

Leaders are constantly bombarded with issues, all of which seem to require attention and resources. But are the leaders choosing the right problems? This question targets what we call *problem uncertainty*. In any situation, most participants and observers have an incomplete or inaccurate picture of what is going on and what is at issue. And we all tend to overvalue information that is consistent with our existing beliefs. The sheer volume of information that leaders must consider, process, and interpret amplifies these problems.[3] Efficiency demands and performance demands can make matters worse by prompting leaders to stop searching for solutions once they find one that seems "good enough."[4]

One way to tackle problem uncertainty is to solicit as much feedback as possible as quickly as possible from the most diverse possible array of individuals. Some experts argue that it is best to consult an organized focus group, and to space out its feedback. According to this way of thinking, using a focus group improves proficiency and the likelihood of acquiring targeted feedback from knowledgeable consumers. Spacing out feedback allows more time for reflection and review after each interaction, and thus avoids cognitive overload. Intermittent feedback also allows the interweaving of advice with experimentation, enabling leaders to iterate between receiving advice and implementing it for testing purposes.[5] Spacing out feedback may be especially appropriate to innovation: doing so allows leaders sufficient time to develop insight into the various elements of novel business models.[6]

Our research shows otherwise. We found that an unorganized, unfocused array of people is preferable to a focus group because the diversity of input exposes biases and blind spots embedded in the existing problem definition and framing, which in turn helps leaders cast their net more accurately in the search for a solution.[7] Our research also suggests that amassing lots of input upfront is more helpful than receiving feedback over an extended span of time: patterns are more evident when feedback is solicited within a compressed period of time. At some organizations we researched, innovators were meeting with sixty-five to seventy-five people over a span of three weeks to get feedback on their ideas. At one firm, a leader eager to innovate met with fifty-four people in the space of thirty days. Such *compression of feedback* showcases consistent and compelling evidence of patterns that is hard to overlook or dismiss. For example, feedback from many individuals within a brief span might make a strong case that leaders are spending too much time on an issue unworthy of such effort and expense. Conversely, a pattern in concentrated feedback might indicate that leaders are devoting too little time to a compelling value proposition.

What's more, collecting lots of information from an unorganized, unfocused array of people forces leaders to keep exploring, and to look further afield for solutions that fit their business model and strategy. In other words, getting lots of input upfront acts as a forcing mechanism: it obliges leaders to search more deeply and more broadly for improvements to dimensions of their business model or strategy that they might otherwise have viewed as satisfactory. One leader at a new venture in the United States told us that early feedback helped his team realize they were focusing on the wrong problem:

> We had a plan to look like a distributor for [industry] and take inventory. We very quickly took that off our list of to-dos [when we learned that it is] a

horrible business. . . . We started realizing the problem isn't just selling stuff to these people; the problem is they don't even know how to do these projects themselves. So we said that, for them to be successful in their contract businesses, all these small businesses need technology to automate the way they do business. And that's how we backed into building software to support independent small businesses.[8]

Inviting as much feedback as possible as quickly as possible from an unfocused array of people might look like drinking from a firehose. But it can work wonders: compressed feedback pushes leaders to overcome their own and others' biases by considering more dimensions of the problem and a wider range of strategic considerations before trying to construct a solution.[9] It also helps leaders overcome their known and unknown biases by providing them a form of social proof, one that takes shape when feedback from multiple dissimilar individuals converges in a way that implicitly challenges the primacy of the leader's own opinion.[10] Thus, more compressed interaction with a diverse array of individuals improves the reliability of what is learned through data triangulation. That is, any finding or conclusion carries more weight and is likely to be more convincing if it is based on the pooling of several distinct but confirmatory sources of information.[11] Moreover, because compressed feedback is fresh and memorable, it is less likely to be dismissed, especially when many differently situated individuals agree.

When, by contrast, feedback is more intermittent, leaders tend to try to implement each individual's advice. This reaction can result in operational and strategic zigzagging, and even impulsive pivoting or failure to address something important. One leader received such scattered feedback that she later recalled overresponding to "every person's piece of feedback—and that led to way too many changes for me and my team." Every couple of weeks they built a new version of a project, without gaining traction or decisively moving forward on any of them.

Using Crowds to Test Whether You've Found the Right Solutions

Once leaders are confident that they are solving the right problem (*problem uncertainty*), they will need to tackle *demand uncertainty* in a similar way. Demand uncertainty refers to lack of knowledge about whether people will want your solution. Will they buy it? Will they use it? Will they share it with others? A good way to approach demand uncertainty is to design for extreme users—that is, for individuals who are deeply invested in the problem you are trying to solve. A number of historically transformative innovations have begun as designs for extreme users. In the nineteenth century, the Italian inventor Pellegrino Turi created a workaround to help his nearly blind mother write letters more easily and legibly. His solution spawned the typewriter, which in turn became the foundation for computer keyboard design.[12] Likewise, Alexander Graham Bell's personal interest in the education of people who are deaf prompted him to invent the microphone and, in 1876, what he called an "electrical speech machine," which became the telephone.[13]

Designing for extreme users helps leaders grasp the full spectrum of users and use cases (which can be surprising).[14] Extreme users can be both super-users and nonusers; their challenges tend to be intensified versions of those faced by mainstream users. The heightened sensitivities of both power users and avoidant users help leaders recognize and examine the causes of particular use cases and workarounds, and recognize and better connect with both groups' needs, beliefs, and desires. Furthermore, an offering that is attractive to an extreme user can often be generalized for a larger mainstream audience confronting similar challenges in a less intense way. Designers at Ford outfitted test drivers with bodysuits to simulate the experience of elderly drivers, who tend to be less agile: a button or a switch whose inconvenient placement merely annoys a forty-year-old might be out of reach for an eighty-year-old. This usability-centered approach led to new features, such as easier-to-reach seatbelts, that benefited all drivers. Similarly, Nintendo tapped a surprising group of extreme users—people who hate playing video games—when designing its Wii gaming console. Their insights prompted the design team to create a console that responded to people's natural movements, a welcome change for gamers and technologists of all stripes. More recently, extreme usership helped shape Twitter. In Twitter's early days, one extreme user, Chris Messina, pointed out that the platform didn't organize topics coherently. In blogs and posts, he urged users to adopt the hashtag symbol as a way to organize their posts topically. The Twitter team resisted the hashtag symbol, considering it too nerdy. Messina continued pushing for its adoption. Eventually his efforts paid off; the hashtag symbol took hold and is now a mainstream feature of Twitter.

Extreme users are often outliers strongly committed to proposed products or services. As such, we can think of them as "the love group"—users who can be counted on to recommend their favorite products and services freely without being asked. Lee Redden and Jorge Heraud of Blue River Technology initially envisioned building automated lawnmowers for golf courses, which typically feature different types of grass of differing heights in different spots. But when their sales pitches met with a tepid response, Redden and Heraud realized that their technology solved a nonexistent problem: golf courses already had lawnmowers, operated by expert landscapers, that could be adjusted to cut grass at different heights. Blue River's technology was thus both redundant and expensive relative to existing solutions. But by continuing to talk to potential customers, the pair discovered that farmers would welcome their technology: it would help them treat weeds and crops differently across hundreds of acres of land. Redden and Heraud had found their love group. They quickly built and tested a new prototype customized for farmers' needs and pain points. Within nine months they had raised more than $3 million in financing; nine months later, they had a commercial product purposefully designed to help farmers in California's Central Valley get better yields on lettuce.

All too often, innovators, convinced they need to scale up quickly, focus on the mass market rather than on a smaller love group. By scaling up quickly, they reason, they will gain a larger market share and grow faster, both desirable outcomes in industries dominated by direct and indirect network effects and winner-take-all dynamics. In reality, though, most startups fail because they scale up too quickly. An analysis of 3,200 startups performed by Startup Genome found that 70 percent failed because of premature scaling up: trying to grow the business before nailing the product and market fit. In retrospect, the mistake seems obvious; less obvious is why leaders make the mistake at all. Innovators, it seems, often take the right steps in the wrong order.

Many hew closely to a path they learned in business school: hit on a high-demand idea, build a solution that will satisfy demand, bring in experienced people to sell the solution, and create marketing materials to promote it. What many innovators lose sight of is that they are pursuing a mere idea—an unclear solution for an unclear market. It usually takes two to three times longer than leaders expect to achieve product fit, and before then, scaling up isn't appropriate. Premature scaling up often leads to a depletion of cash, which makes it harder for leaders to adjust when unexpected early problems arise. Scaling up too quickly also makes shifting gears more difficult. Leaders become wedded to a particular solution. As they increase investments in people and processes to promote that solution, their commitment escalates further, making it even more difficult to turn back.

When dealing with demand uncertainty, it is counterintuitive to *do things that don't scale up*. But our research led us to precisely that insight: leaders should first identify a love group, probe its members' unique wants, and then overdeliver for them. By doing so, leaders will gain penetrating insights into the highest-priority issues of their happiest users—individuals who are knowledgeable and willing to experiment to satisfy their unmet needs. Such individuals often become the earliest adopters without realizing it. They can then be used as surrogates for future users and later adopters. In the absence of this kind of clarity, teams tend to encounter confusion and frustration. With such clarity, innovating firms often thrive: boosted by the evangelism of early users, they free up budgets to help teams execute guided by more precise performance metrics. And by overdelivering for one group, leaders often find they have created something that many other people want.

The Honda Ridgeline, a pickup truck, embodies the value of enlisting extreme users and love groups to help address demand uncertainty. To gear up for design of the Ridgeline, Honda staff spoke about form and functionality with people who loved their pickup trucks. They asked people who ran their businesses out of their pickups, such as electricians, plumbers, gardeners, auto detailers, and general contractors, about gas mileage, the cab interior, dial layouts, and other hardware. Then they asked which of all these considerations was the most important. The answer: the tailgate. A traditional truck opens by pulling down the tailgate; these users wanted greater functionality, such as a tailgate that would both detach and swing out to allow easier manipulation of cargo. Honda engineers responded to these use cases, which they probably would not have imagined otherwise, by designing just such a tailgate for the new pickup.

The team also addressed demand uncertainty by reaching out to another extreme group, buyers who barely used their pickups at all. These customers enjoyed using the pickup bed as a buffet station when entertaining friends at tailgate parties before sporting events. Honda responded by incorporating an easy-to-drain ice cooler into the bed of the Ridgeline; an electrical outlet was added for appliances like TVs, generators, and cocktail mixers. By interacting with both sets of extreme users—those whose work depended on their pickups and those who used them largely as party-mobiles—Honda turned a good pickup into one of the most popular trucks in America. In 2017–2018 more than 40,000 Ridgelines were sold in the United States, or one in every ten midsize trucks sold. The Ridgeline lured customers away from the Chevrolet Colorado, the GMC Canyon, and the Toyota Tacoma, and even attracted new customers who ordinarily bought sedans like the Honda Accord.

It is not widely understood that innovators must take actions early on that do not scale up. That is, they must resist the urge to scale up too quickly and instead take time to fully grasp the needs of extreme users and to test solutions with them. Because of their personal connections to a particular problem, extreme users are less useful earlier on, while innovators are exploring problem uncertainty. But once leaders have focused on the right problem, slowing down to test potential solutions with extreme users will facilitate rapid scaling up later by indirectly addressing the needs of those who will appreciate the same solutions in a less fervent way. In other words, extreme users can help resolve demand uncertainty by expanding the range of use cases to its fullest extent and by identifying aspects of the problem that most need solving. Without calling on extreme users, organizational leaders can easily fall into the trap of designing for the mainstream user. Aiming to please average users—frequently a very diverse group—can result in a generic, average product or service that is both uninspiring and easy to copy.

Using Crowds to Execute Solutions

The third phase of crowd sequencing involves using crowds to execute solutions. In other words, it addresses supply uncertainty. By *supply uncertainty*, we mean that even after you've figured out what people want, it isn't clear that your organization can actually supply it. That is, do you have the knowledge and understanding necessary to create (i.e., to supply) what is in demand? Executing a new solution, especially one dependent on a new technology, typically means solving a series of new problems that call for bits and pieces of know-how from an array of sources. Though leaders are inclined at this juncture to consult their closest associates for ideas and expertise, a better approach is to reach out to people they barely know. Established teams are liable to revert to the same old approaches. When seeking the kinds of novel solutions that executing a new product or service tends to require, it makes sense to look beyond your usual networks and tap people in other departments or even other organizations.

When it comes to accessing novel information and knowledge— which leaders need to do to innovate quickly and frugally—*weak ties* are usually the most valuable. Close associates are apt to know what leaders already know. Activating and leveraging weak ties can give leaders access to the fresh ideas, resources, and expertise needed to implement novel solutions that users want. Sociologist Mark Granovetter spelled out this counterintuitive insight in a 1973 paper provocatively titled "The Strength of Weak Ties."[15] Granovetter set out to pinpoint the ties that prove most useful when searching for a new job. Conventional wisdom at the time was that your closest connections would be most likely to help you get a job. But the central challenge in the job market is typically uncovering an open position in the first place. Granovetter found that weak ties are more likely to know about jobs you are not already aware of.

The benefit of leveraging weak ties is exemplified by a multinational computer company[16] where engineers on different teams learned from each other. Some sets of teams already had strong ties because they frequently interacted; others rarely if ever did so. An internal study revealed that engineers from units with weaker ties learned from each other more effectively, and so were much quicker to create solutions, while units with preexisting strong ties had a harder time pinpointing the knowledge they needed, which delayed completion time dramatically.

The technology giant Canon leveraged weak ties to develop the AE-1, the world's first electronically controlled, fully automatic, single lens reflex (SLR) camera with a built-in microprocessor unit. Employees familiar with precision optics and camera mechanics were assigned to work with others knowledgeable about miniaturized electronic circuitry developed for handheld calculators. Few had worked together before, but the resulting cross-fertilization of technical know-how benefited the novel SLR. Similarly, Canon developed its personal copier by connecting experts in photocopying processes with experts in chemistry. Jointly, the two groups created a typewriter-size copier with an easy-to-replace disposable toner cartridge, a new product that was soon in high demand.

The point is to promote greater diversity in personal networks in order to generate a variety of novel options for executing ideas.[17] Small organizational interventions to foster weak personal network ties can have big results. Google deliberately scatters its cafeterias around its campus and encourages employees to avoid habitually frequenting the nearest one. Doing so gives organizational members multiple places to bump into one another, increasing the chances that people from different departments will meet, chat, and discover how they (or friends in their network) might help one another.

Pixar did something similar. When Steve Jobs designed Pixar's corporate offices in the late 1980s, he had architects locate the cafés, mailboxes, and restrooms in the atrium rather than in the usual side corridors so that employees who wouldn't normally interact would bump into each other. Indeed, such encounters led to spontaneous chatter and frequently to useful solutions.[18] What can leaders do now that the physical office seems likely to be less relevant in the workplace of the future? If organizations will be increasingly defined by teams working both on-site and remotely, such spontaneous encounters may become even more important for collaborative tasks. Though employees who work remotely say they are at least as productive at individual tasks, such as analyzing data, writing presentations, and executing administrative tasks, as when they are on-site, they have a harder time with tasks that require working with others, including exchanges with co-workers, working in teams, and interacting with clients.[19] For those working remotely, leaders can create opportunities for spontaneous encounters on digital platforms by arranging for frequent informal communication and encouraging off-site presentations and get-togethers.

In summary, tackling supply uncertainty frequently requires the help of people we know only superficially or not at all. Most individuals' connections are limited to their immediate sphere. The challenge, then, is to tap into weak ties among groups of people who aren't currently connected but who jointly possess the skills, perspective, and know-how to implement a given solution.

Conclusion

Accelerating innovation calls for making use of those around us in quick and easy ways. Crowd sequencing entails leveraging a variety of crowds, both groups external to and those inside the organization, in different phases of an entrepreneurial initiative to address different types of uncertainty (see figure 4.1). Just as sequencing is essential when building a house or baking a cake, so too is it essential when enlisting others in pursuit of innovation.

1. PROBLEM UNCERTAINTY

- ❖ Who: An unfocused array of people
- ❖ How: Compress feedback

2. DEMAND UNCERTAINTY

- ❖ Who: A love group
- ❖ How: Overdeliver for extreme users and do things that don't scale up

3. SUPPLY UNCERTAINTY

- ❖ Who: Weak ties
- ❖ How: Create interventions to increase diversity in personal networks

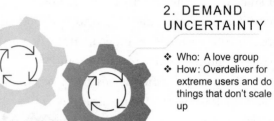

Figure 4.1

Table 4.1
The benefits of crowd sequencing

Instead of doing this . . .	Do this . . .	And get this result . . .
Crowdsourcing	Use crowd sequencing.	Accelerated innovation, by leveraging knowledge inside and outside the organization
Soliciting feedback from a focus group	Temporally compress feedback from an unfocused array of individuals.	A higher likelihood of recognizing patterns in feedback that can help resolve problem uncertainty ("Are w focused on the right thing?")
Finding many users who like your product or service to aid rapid scaling up	Pursue activities that don't scale up: overdeliver for a few people who love your product or service and use them as stand-ins for future customers.	A higher likelihood of addressing demand uncertainty ("Do we know who will adopt, use, promote, or pay for our product or service?") by freei up budgets to help teams execute guided by more precise specification
Drawing on strong-tie relationships to execute a project	Leverage weak ties.	A higher likelihood of addressing supply uncertainty ("Can we provid what customers want?") by gaining access to fresh ideas, resources, and expertise

5 Rational Heuristics: The "Simple Rules" That Leaders Use to Simplify Complexity

Complexity, in the technical sense of the term, exists whenever a system has multiple interdependent parts. A two-person startup is less complex than a ten-person team and a ten-person team is less complex than a two hundred-person organization. As organizations evolve, and complexity inevitably grows, leaders adopt policies and procedures to impose order and increase efficiency. The problem is that, over time, the accumulation of such structure further increases complexity. Think of the compliance departments of large firms in regulated industries or the layers of policies and procedures that a typical university administrator must understand and navigate. Increased complexity stemming from the natural accretion of structure also makes organizations less flexible and more bureaucratic—a distressingly common state of affairs. Indeed, nearly two-thirds of respondents to a survey by *Harvard Business Review* reported that their organizations had become more bureaucratic in recent years.[1] To counteract drift toward increased bureaucracy—a particularly serious problem for organizations in fast-moving, uncertain environments that require agility and adaptation—savvy leaders employ *heuristics*. Heuristics are simple rules of thumb that individuals can rely on, in preference to comprehensive information and analysis, to streamline decision-making. We find that these heuristics are deliberately created by organizational members based on experience and then used as condensed statements of strategy.

Berkshire Hathaway, for example, relies on a few rules of thumb when selecting businesses to acquire: (1) large purchases (at least $50 million in before-tax earnings), (2) no turnarounds, and (3) little or no debt. Samsung adheres to a simple rule of thumb by regularly releasing new phones twice a year, in early spring and fall. At a more granular level, Chick-Fil-A relies on rules of thumb to guide customer service. Whenever a guest says "Thank you," a Chick-Fil-A team member responds "My pleasure!" (not "You're welcome!"). And, as COVID-19 began to spread globally, most Americans became familiar with Dr. Anthony Fauci's three rules of thumb for physical distancing: (1) stay six feet apart, (2) limit gatherings to ten or fewer people, and (3) wear a mask in the presence of people other than members of your own household.

Most research on heuristics emphasizes the cognitive errors such rules of thumb can produce: recency bias, a focus on nonrepresentative data, misuse of probability, and the like. This orientation treats heuristics as handy but poor substitutes for computations that are too intricate to perform regularly. Indeed, Daniel Kahneman was awarded the 2002 Nobel Memorial Prize in Economic Sciences largely for his work on commonplace cognitive errors that arise from reliance on universal heuristics in decision-making.[2] Many leaders have adopted this largely negative stance, blaming heuristics for irrational behavior and strategic failure. But our analysis of successful strategies on the part of leaders in dynamic environments found the opposite, namely, that heuristics appear to be central to high performance.[3] The purpose of this chapter is to demonstrate that adhering to simple rules is often the most effective strategy in complex environments. Not only is it often effective strategy to employ heuristics, their content is often strategic in nature, too. First we explain how heuristics can help (rather than hurt) organizations. We then specify the specific (not universal) types of heuristics that leaders should create. Finally, we spell out how leaders can keep their rules of thumb from becoming bureaucratic.

How Can Heuristics Help (Rather Than Hurt) Organizations?

Much experimental work on heuristics employs problems that are not strategically relevant (e.g., binary-choice questions with correct answers)[4] and restricts opportunities for study participants to learn. In other words, by relying on unrealistic contexts, research often stacks the deck against heuristics. Even so, we argue that heuristics are a rational approach to decisions in situations characterized by highly heterogeneous individual experience and high unpredictability—both of which are attributes of most dynamic environments.

1. Simple-rule heuristics are useful because they help leaders negotiate the fundamental tension between efficiency and flexibility. Easy-to-use rules of thumb accelerate decision-making and simplify problem solving by restricting the scope of possible solutions; doing so in turn improves efficiency. But by not specifying the details of the solution, heuristics leave room for flexible action. Consider Amazon's "two-pizza teams" rule: if two pizzas aren't enough to feed a team, according to CEO Jeff Bezos, the team is too big. This simple rule is both efficient and flexible. It's efficient because it's easy to remember and apply; it also reduces demands on employees' time and makes decision-making less bureaucratic. The rule is flexible, too: it doesn't dictate who should be on the team, what team members should talk about, or for how long. In other words, simple-rule heuristics are strict but not restrictive.

2. Simple-rule heuristics are useful because they're easy to remember and to share across a geographically dispersed workforce. The business accelerator Y Combinator uses a few simple rules to run its program for startup founders: (1) a duration of three months, (2) a single location (Menlo Park), (3) $20,000 for each startup that joins the program, in exchange for 6–8 percent in equity, and (4) a requirement that the founders be physically present. Such easy-to-remember rules are also easy to follow and implement. Research shows that knowledge retention is enhanced when lessons are simple: the capacity limitations of short-term memory restrict the amount of information that can be encoded in long-term memory. Simplicity also makes lessons easier to remember even when individuals are tired, stressed, and anxious.

3. Simple-rule heuristics provide value because they're cheap and surprisingly on-target. Analytically complex, information-intensive approaches often underperform because they try to accommodate

every situation, weight diverse information ineffectively, and fail to exploit people's existing knowledge of the context.[5] For example, in a study of how investors make decisions using comparably sound approaches, scholars found that investors who made use of a single heuristic—invest equally in all asset classes—outperformed investment strategies that relied on substantially more information, analysis, and computation.[6] Similarly, in a study of how individuals solve serial crimes, scholars found that those who applied a single heuristic— look for suspects at the midpoint between the two most distant crime scenes—found the perpetrator more quickly and accurately than did those who used a complex computational approach.[7] Additionally, relying on high-effort information-intensive approaches can lead individuals to make choices they later regret because they focused too much attention on less relevant details.[8]

In sum, when environments become more complex, the best strategies are often the simplest. Thus, effective leaders in dynamic environments develop a few simple-rule heuristics that provide some structure—such that they can efficiently build on the past—but not too much structure to flexibly adapt in the present.

What Specific (Not Universal) Types of Heuristics Should Leaders Adopt?

Prior research has identified several universal heuristics, such as representativeness and availability, that individuals use to find answers to binary-choice problems (e.g., "Does Cologne have a larger population than Bonn?"). The key insight here is that individuals tend to rely automatically on universal rules of thumb to make judgments, though such rules often produce systematic errors (biases) precisely because they are cognitively easy to use. For example, Kahneman noted that, when guessing an individual's occupation, most people ignore general information on prevalence in favor of stereotypes: a person described as mild and quiet tends to be identified as a librarian, not a farmer, though farmers outnumber librarians in the general population by a factor of twenty.[9] The author attributes this judgment error to the "representativeness" heuristic, or reliance on common stereotypes to make choices. Likewise, Kahneman and Tversky asked study subjects whether the letter k is more likely to be the first or the third letter in a word. Most people intuitively use the availability heuristic and answer "first"—that is, words that begin with the letter in question come more quickly to mind (i.e., are more readily available) than words in which it appears later. Yet the correct answer for k is third.[10]

Our subject here is the heuristics that are particular to organizations. By analyzing many sets of heuristics used in dynamic settings characterized by unpredictability (as opposed to binary-choice problems with correct answers), we discerned that organizations typically create several types of heuristics. We designate these types (1) *selection heuristics*, which help to distinguish between activities to pursue and those to ignore; (2) *procedure heuristics*, which guide the execution of selected activities; (3) *priority heuristics*, which help rank activities; and (4) *timing heuristics*, which guide the sequencing and pacing of activities.

Selection heuristics define what organizations or teams will and will not look into. By setting boundaries—by specifying what to pursue and what to ignore—leaders narrow the range of possible actions. For example, leaders might use selection heuristics to restrict the development of new products to retail software, excluding both financial products and low-cost products. Leaders might also use selection heuristics to target specific customer types (e.g., large financial institutions or telecom operators) or specific locations (e.g., Asia, big cities, Scandinavia). In short, selection heuristics specify which opportunities and activities to explore and which to ignore. For instance, executives at Tanger, a North Carolina–based real estate investment trust, created selection heuristics to help choose locations for future retail outlets. To meet Tanger's criteria, a potential location had to have the following characteristics: (1) be suitable for an outdoor-type shopping center, (2) have a population of at least one million within a thirty- to forty-mile radius, and (3) have an average household income in excess of $65,000. Without selection heuristics, leaders can waste time chasing unpromising opportunities, or become overwhelmed by so many options that they fail to act at all. The end result—too much flexibility and too little structure—can resemble the opportunistic approach to opportunity selection discussed in chapter 1 on the opportunity paradox. Leading in such a scenario, without a plan, can also frustrate and confuse staff.

Procedure heuristics specify the actions that an organization should take to pursue a given activity. Procedure heuristics are deliberate rules of thumb that typically draw on the know-how and experience of leaders and staff. Leaders at the In-N-Out Burger restaurant chain, for example, adopted several procedure heuristics to guide operations: (1) do not sell or use frozen beef patties (which helps ensure that customers get only high-quality meat); (2) serve only hand-cut fries (meaning they aren't frozen either) and bake fresh buns each day; and (3) do not equip any restaurant locations with freezers or microwaves. Like selection heuristics, procedure heuristics focus attention on ways to maintain quality and avoid missteps. Leaders at Raindance, an independent film festival and film school, compiled several procedure heuristics for writing award-winning short films: (1) the shorter the better (fifteen seconds to forty-five minutes); (2) make it visual; that is, tell the story with images; (3) tell a compelling story; that is, engage the audience; and (4) beware of clichés: avoid such stereotypes as hitmen for hire, heists, and children as embodiments of innocence unless you have a novel twist.[11]

Priority heuristics rank an organization's most important activities and opportunities, helping to allocate resources rationally. Some examples: "Enter regions with the highest mobile penetration first," "Start with the automotive sector," or "Enter English-speaking markets first." Often priority heuristics improve ongoing allocation of resources among *simultaneous* activities. In 2004, prior to their IPO, Google cofounders Larry Page and Sergey Brin created the 20 percent rule, which encouraged Google employees to spend 20 percent of their time on nonformal, discretionary projects. The cofounders wrote, "We encourage our employees, in addition to their regular projects, to spend 20 percent of their time working on what they think will most benefit Google." One of these innovations was Gmail. According to a Google spokesperson, the 20 percent time rule is "a long-standing Google initiative . . . and still an active program."[12] Similarly, in 2005, immediately after Google's IPO, when the core search business was growing rapidly, then CEO Eric Schmidt and cofounders Larry Page and Sergey Brin realized that refining Google's search engine would consume too many resources (time, money, employees), resulting in merely incremental innovation. To ensure that Google would invest in both incremental and disruptive innovation, they added the 70/20/10 rule for formal (nondiscretionary) work assignments: 70 percent of employees' aggregate time should be dedicated to Google's core business, 20 percent to projects adjacent to the core business, and 10 percent to projects unrelated to the core business (e.g., driverless vehicles). Google's leaders stressed the importance of the rule. By adhering to this heuristic, they said, employees would generate more original ideas—Google employees were often accused of creating copycat ideas—in all of the company's businesses (core, adjacent, and disruptive) and distinguish the business from its competitors. Firms that lack priority heuristics may allocate resources to the wrong activities or pursue too many opportunities at once, while failing to profit significantly from any single opportunity.

By providing direction about how to use and structure time, *timing heuristics* impose a rhythm on activity and interaction. Some organizational leaders restrict when meetings can be scheduled (no meetings after lunch, for example, to let employees devote their afternoons to uninterrupted work). Elon Musk created several timing heuristics for meetings at Tesla and SpaceX: (1) keep meetings short, typically thirty minutes or less; (2) make the base frequency of meetings match the urgency of the matter at hand; and (3) leave a meeting if you think you are not adding value. Leaders at Detroit-based Quicken Loans also adopted a simple but effective timing heuristic: every phone call or email message from a customer must be returned on the day it's received, even if it arrives as an employee is leaving for the day. Dan Gilbert, the company's founder, zealously adheres to this rule of thumb; he has been known to give new employees his phone number so that he can call a customer back if the new recruit is too busy. Even now that the business has become the largest US mortgage lender, it maintains this heuristic. Customers seem to appreciate it: in 2019, Quicken Loans earned J.D. Power's highest rating for client satisfaction among all US mortgage lenders for the tenth year in a row.

Timing heuristics can make a decisive difference in unpredictable environments, where capturing fleeting opportunities can mean the difference between success and failure. Companies that lack timing heuristics may change too much, too little, or in the wrong order. Simple timing heuristics specify when staff should act; they can thus help synchronize the efforts of separate departments (e.g., sales, engineering, and marketing), or help an organization synchronize with its environment by linking it to its market and to prevailing product development and sales cycles. One of Apple's timing heuristics, for example, is to release new products in the fall, usually in September, to benefit from the back-to-school rush and to get a jump on holiday sales.

Though we have found the typology of organizations' heuristics to be remarkably consistent from one organization to another, their specific content is often idiosyncratic. For example, many of the firms we studied adopted procedure heuristics for entering new markets, but the precise details of those rules of thumb varied—some were aimed at direct sales, for instance, while others targeted indirect sales, even when the firms were entering the same markets.

Another key insight is that organizational heuristics have a common structure. Leaders translate their experience into specific types of heuristics (i.e., selection, procedure, priority, and timing) that are consistent across organizations. This structure of heuristics exists because of the underlying problem that organizational growth often addresses—the effective capture of unique opportunities within a larger flow of heterogeneous possibilities. For example, Google aims to make high-performing acquisitions from a large pool of heterogeneous candidates; Volkswagen attempts to choose partnerships from a large pool of high-performing, heterogeneous potential partners; Lyft chooses which countries to enter next from a large pool of possibilities. Selection heuristics help firms cope with such abundance by constraining the range of opportunities. Similarly, procedure heuristics constrain how growth-pursuing processes such as country entry should proceed, thus speeding action, conserving attention, and improving the reliability of opportunity capture. Similarly, priority heuristics guide leaders to avoid acceptable but lower-value opportunities in favor of higher-value alternatives. And because capturing growth opportunities typically requires internal coordination of limited resources, timing heuristics that specify a sequence or a pace can be advantageous.[13]

Keeping Simple Rules Simple

What happens to heuristics over time? We found that good executive teams tend to elaborate the number and detail of their heuristics as they gain experience, which makes for increasingly comprehensive and up-to-date heuristic portfolios. But better executive teams both elaborate and simplify their heuristic portfolios. That is, they prune their heuristic portfolios as they gain experience. In short, effectively simplifying complexity requires managing both the type and the number of an organization's heuristics (see figure 5.1).

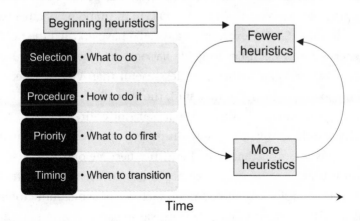

Figure 5.1

Our research on a US-based enterprise-software firm illustrates the process of simplification. The founders created customer relationship management (CRM) software to help client firms mine their data. During the firm's first two country entries, into Australia and the UK, the executive team relied on a few selection heuristics (e.g., "restrict internationalization to English-speaking markets" and "sell real-time analytics") and a few procedure heuristics (e.g., "use implementation partners" and "have a person at HQ devoted to liaison with the team in a foreign country"). But the executive team then jettisoned the heuristic to expand into only English-speaking markets: executives had perceived that the language restriction closed off attractive opportunities in non-English-speaking markets such as France, Germany, and Korea, which became the company's next three entries. Rather than substituting a priority heuristic (e.g., "give preference to English-speaking markets") or elaborating the original selection heuristic (e.g., "enter English-speaking and/or large markets"), the executive team simplified the firm's heuristics portfolio by eliminating it altogether. The executive team also eliminated the procedure heuristic "have a person at HQ devoted to liaison with the team in a foreign country" because executives had observed that liaison activities consumed too much leadership time. As a HQ leader noted, "It wasn't really until after we entered the country that I realized what a huge job I had to do in headquarters to keep the U.K. and Australia in the mind-set of other senior leaders in the U.S." The executive team could have updated the heuristic or generated new heuristics to guide liaisons' activities. Instead, having realized that liaison activities were less useful than granting decision-making power to the in-country staff, the executive team simplified its heuristic portfolio by eliminating that heuristic entirely.

Why should leaders purposely prune their portfolios of heuristics? An obvious reason is that some heuristics become obsolete. A subtler reason is that firms often replace naive early heuristics with strategic ones. For example, a US-based manufacturer of semiconductor solutions for GPS-enabled mobile devices was expanding internationally; one of its procedure heuristics specified using Taiwan for design of the firm's chips and China for manufacturing. As one executive explained, "Initially, we thought the product should be designed in Taiwan and manufactured in China because of the cheap labor." But after entering China, the executive team realized that China was preferable for both manufacturing and design owing to the growing technological capabilities found in the country: "What we found out," the CEO noted, "is that our design activity should be in China and the manufacturing should also be in China." This learning prompted the executive team to substitute the earlier heuristic for a better one that was far more pertinent to success: use China for both design and manufacturing. The firm also used this heuristic to guide the execution of subsequent country entries.

In other circumstances, leaders have replaced granular heuristics with more abstract ones; for example, executives at a data analytics company in Singapore replaced the selection heuristic "Sell to governments, insurance companies, and banks" with "Sell to organizations with extensive proprietary data and ability to pay." This heuristic led the firm to target oil companies in Saudi Arabia, insurance firms in Malaysia, state-owned enterprises in China, and manufacturing firms in Japan. Other firms have done the opposite, adopting more precise heuristics, such as priority heuristics to focus on particular markets, services, or products.

As for why organizations keep their heuristics portfolios small, our research suggests an intriguing explanation: a fundamental trade-off between adding new heuristics to efficiently address every situation versus making do with a few heuristics in conjunction with real-time problem solving. Too many rules, even simple ones, can create confusion and even inconsistency. On the other hand, eliminating too many rules can risk erasing the lessons of past experience and result in mistakes. The process of simplification—the mental exercise of deciding what to simplify and how—helps balance this tension. Leaders should aim to compile a portfolio of rules thorough enough for people to become accustomed to relying on it to reduce mistakes but compact enough to leave room for flexible action.[14]

In general, the process of adding and pruning heuristics ensures their efficient encoding in leaders' long-term memory, for easy recall and better updating. By maintaining a small heuristic portfolio, executives can achieve a balance between gaining traction and efficiency through consistent actions (e.g., "always use partners") and maintaining the flexibility to improvise (e.g., "adopt country-specific approaches to finding partners"). Thus, firms should avoid "overfitting" heuristics to accommodate the specifics of every opportunity. Further, this advice is consistent with findings that experts constantly fine-tune their mental models[15]: as expertise increases, guidelines tend to become fewer, more strategic, and increasingly abstract.[16]

In an effort to keep simple rules simple, leaders should regularly ask themselves and their teams two questions: (1) Do we have procedures, processes, or policies that can be eliminated? (2) Do we require routine steps or actions that can be omitted to move more quickly and efficiently? Often the answer to both questions is yes. Even simple rules can outlive their usefulness.

Conclusion

Successful leaders in dynamic environments compile *portfolios of heuristics*. Accustomed to approaching unpredictable and complex situations as problem solvers, they generate heuristics suited to the available information (often spotty) and to available attention (often time-limited) but that nevertheless provide workable solutions that are amenable to improvement. Because such heuristics are by definition easy to access and remember, they are readily communicated to and understood by widely dispersed firm members. Is there an ideal number of heuristics in a portfolio? No. Simple rules should be kept simple, yet three to eight rules is a rough target range.[17] Remember, however, that such rules apply to a particular process (e.g., onboarding, fundraising, partnering); they are not mission statements or vision statements, which apply to everything the organization does.

Further, we found heuristics to have a *uniform structure* but unique content. That is, the four types of heuristics—selection, procedure, priority, and timing—are consistent across organizations but the specifics differ sufficiently to embody a given organization's unique strategy for competing and winning in its industry. Having all four types of rules is valuable; each addresses a different facet of strategy, namely, what to do, how to do it, what to do first, and how to move from one thing to another. Thus, having all four types helps ensure a more complete and robust strategy.

Successful leaders also engage in *simplification*: they add new heuristics but then prune the portfolio (see table 5.1). By maintaining a small heuristic portfolio, executives can achieve a balance between consistency and sufficient flexibility to improvise. Heuristics thus encapsulate the active, pragmatic approaches of effective problem solvers who must contend with spotty information, limited time and attention, and too many opportunities. In other words, heuristics are simple rules that leaders use to simplify complexity and to support rational strategy in dynamic settings.

Table 5.1
A guide to using simple heuristics

Instead of . . .	Do this . . .	And get this result . . .
Viewing heuristics as biased and dysfunctional, leading to errors in decision-making	Treat heuristics as a rational approach to decision-making in dynamic environments.	Improved organizational alignment, engagement, and adaptation
Seeking heuristics that are equally applicable to all organizations or unique to a single organization	Develop heuristics that are specific in their details but share a typology (i.e., selection, procedure, priority, and timing) with those of other organizations.	A differentiated but comprehensive and robust strategy, since each type of heuristic addresses a particular aspect of strategy (what to do, how to do it, what to do first, and when to proceed from one activity to the next)
Accumulating many heuristics as experience accumulates	Simplify and prune existing heuristics.	A portfolio of heuristics large enough to rely on by providing efficient guidance but compact and flexible enough to accommodate a wide range of action

III   Engaging with Stakeholders

6 Framing Innovations Effectively: Making the New Familiar, Then Novel

In the early 1970s, Americans barely ate sushi. The notion of eating raw fish seemed strange, foreign, and vaguely repulsive. Then the California roll came along. Its most conspicuous ingredients—avocado, cucumber, and rice—were entirely familiar; its slightly more exotic component, crabmeat, was tucked inside a tidy package that even the least adventurous American would be willing to try. The California roll became a gateway introduction to sushi.[1] People soon felt comfortable trying other kinds of sushi, and the rest is history. Sushi restaurants, which had catered almost exclusively to Japanese visitors and Americans of Japanese descent, in a handful of coastal megacities, were soon serving people of all backgrounds in cities and towns across the country. Today Americans consume more than $2 billion worth of sushi every year.

When introducing innovative products and services to prospective consumers, conveying both familiarity and novelty is crucial to success. The story of sushi's spread throughout the United States is a case study in the subtle cultural dynamics that can guide the adoption and diffusion of innovations. Individuals' sense of comfort with a new phenomenon and their attraction to the novelty it represents are the twin determinants of whether they will venture beyond routine and risk giving it a try. No comfort means no willingness; no novelty means no reason to change what you're already doing. Slimy raw fish may be a no-go, but a colorful little roll containing some familiar favorites looks appealing and feels adventurous.

Comfort and attraction, combined in the right proportions, drive new user adoption at the individual level; these individual adoption decisions aggregate over time to create more widespread receptivity. Initial impressions ripple outward through the population, influencing the attitudes of other prospective users. Most people absorb a pervasive consensus that something is interesting or fun or worth trying—or, alternatively, boring or trivial or a waste of time—before they encounter the thing itself. Initially presenting an innovation as familiar, and packaging it in a familiar way, lowers barriers to entry for new users, making the phenomenon simultaneously comprehensible and appealing.[2] If innovators don't emphasize what's familiar, audiences won't feel anchored enough and comfortable enough to give the new thing a chance. But if innovators don't also emphasize what's novel, the attraction and curiosity that drive trial and adoption may never materialize.[3]

How innovation-minded leaders address this tension—when to stress familiarity and when to stress novelty—is central to the success of their organizations. Our research shows that as the speed of (and need for) innovation increases, human perceptions are decisively influential—perhaps even more so than technological benefits—in determining whether new products and services are adopted or rejected. By analyzing the introductions of scores of new technologies and products over the last several decades, we've pinpointed a pattern that explains how successful companies manage the subtle balancing act of framing innovations as *both* familiar and novel. This chapter presents some examples and outlines a simple approach to managing this inherent tension during the critical early stages of an innovation's launch.

During the Earliest Stages of Adoption, Emphasize Familiarity

History demonstrates that people are more accepting of novelty when it is anchored in familiarity—in something that is widely known or widely used.[4] Innovators have long used familiar homespun analogies to encourage consumers to embrace new technologies: automobiles were originally called horseless carriages, and the power generated by automotive engines was (and still is) defined in terms of horsepower.

Such equivalencies helped people grasp the automobile's advantages and made them more comfortable contemplating buying one.[5] Consider the insurance industry's adoption of computers. Insurance workers in the 1950s, encountering computers for the first time, were told that they were a new type of tabulating machine (a device they knew well). The analogy made the computer seem less alien and encouraged them to try it without fear. A more recent example is the internet. Early on, it was sometimes called "the information superhighway," a metaphor intended to emphasize the rapid movement of information from place to place. Emphasis on the technology's simplest capability—fast information transfer—acclimated people gradually to a far more comprehensive innovation, one that involved a global system of interconnected networks that would enable a vast range of information services and resources, such as electronic mail, file sharing, telephony, and commerce.

When Thomas Edison began rolling out the infrastructure and fixtures to electrify American cities, he deliberately designed the new streetlamps to resemble the gas versions he hoped to replace. Thomas A. Edison, Incorporated, buried its wiring underground (much as then existing gas systems were buried), used the same wattage as gas lamps, and retained the familiar meter system to bill customers.[6] Designers and manufacturers of household lamps, picking up on these cues, created electric fixtures that resembled gas fixtures and candelabras.

Similarly, as personal computers proliferated, skeuomorphs—images of familiar physical objects, such as trash bins and shopping carts, to represent digital functions—also proliferated. To make the digital space seem familiar, innovators turned to design cues that deliberately evoked existing materials and services. Apple's novel interface simulated an office environment, complete with a desktop and file folders. The governing idea was to help users feel comfortable in a new world where personal computers would be as commonplace as telephones by equating digital functions with familiar tools. Apple has continued to employ this context-anchoring strategy: its software calendar looks like a desk calendar, its payment options in Apple Wallet look like miniature credit cards, and the calculator app simulates a physical calculator. Reportedly, the Apple design team obsessed over making the Apple Watch's digital knob resemble the knob used to wind up a conventional mechanical watch.

Framing that emphasizes familiarity is especially important when the unfamiliar aspects of a new phenomenon differ sharply from what is currently in use. Maximum alignment between an existing technology and the conceptual frame provided to audiences to interpret the new technology tends to promote its assimilation. A key finding of our research is that, when introducing a new-to-the-world technological innovation, it's wise to begin by emphasizing its similarity to existing technological solutions and minimizing discussion of what is novel.

This principle may seem to be at odds with the prevailing assumption that the source of competitive advantage is distinctiveness. For entrepreneurs introducing new products, that assumption would call for actions that highlight uniqueness to attract attention and set an innovation apart. It may work in an established competitive arena to one-up the competition on features and benefits, but when it comes to introducing something totally new to the world, the risk of focusing on the novel is that prospective customers will fail to grasp the innovation and thus ignore it.

The history of the QR (quick response) code is illustrative. A QR code is a barcode, in the form of a compact square box, that encodes and communicates digital information. Masahiro Hara, a Japanese inventor, and his team at Denso Wave created the QR code in 1994 to improve the company's logistics system and to track inventory; no effort was made at the time to liken it to familiar technologies. Because QR codes use rows and columns to create a grid capable of storing vastly more data than a standard matrix barcode of equivalent size, the QR code could have been framed as "a better barcode." But because it was viewed as too technical for mainstream use, it was never framed this way for public consumption. Thus, even when the QR code was adopted for retail use, the public was largely unaware of the innovation. As recently as 2012, a survey by *Inc.* magazine found that 97 percent of consumers had no idea what a QR code was or when they would ever use one. This state of affairs left the QR code languishing in relative obscurity for decades after its invention. Today the technology is experiencing a modest surge linked to digital activities on apps such as Snapchat, Spotify, and Venmo and services provided by companies such as Alibaba and Amazon, and is seeing increased use in settings where safety, trust, and information privacy are paramount.[7] At a bank or a hospital, for example, touchless digital check-ins with a QR code can ensure greater information privacy than a paper-based system.

A classic example of introducing a new technology to the public by emphasizing its familiar aspects is Niantic's collaboration with Nintendo and The Pokémon Company on the augmented reality (AR) game Pokémon Go. Niantic had developed a high-concept location-based AR game called Ingress in 2012, but its appeal was narrow because few consumers could envision AR as a component of a game played on a phone. The combination of AR and the smartphone was ideal for bridging the digital and physical worlds, but AR was unfamiliar to the public at the time of its release. The concept of venturing around a digital world seeking out mysterious creatures, however, was familiar to an entire generation that had grown up on Pokémon video games and now owned smartphones. Pokémon Go was a perfect vehicle for introducing the possibilities of AR to this audience: instead of a virtual world, you would wander around nearby portions of the actual physical world that Niantic programmers had overlaid with a rich array of digital Pokémon challenges.

As a New Technology Begins to Take Hold, Shift to Emphasizing Its Novelty

Frames that emphasize familiarity facilitate understanding and adoption of new products, systems, and processes, but familiar frames will not excite audiences or attract new users. For a new technology to take hold, it needs to be seen as conceptually distinct from, and better than, the familiar offerings that customers are used to. Our research suggests that dwelling too long on the familiar exacts the cost of failing to draw attention to the novel—that is, to what is new, fresh, and unique. It is novelty, after all, that attracts new audiences and creates new markets.

Thus we arrive at another best practice: as a new technology or product begins to take hold, emphasize its novel aspects. Once barriers to new user adoption have been toppled by invoking analogies that illustrate likely use cases, customers will be ready to focus on the features of the innovation that distinguish it from its predecessors.

When innovators fail to distinguish their innovation from its precursors, audiences are apt to ignore it and continue using existing solutions. An example of this phenomenon is Ethereum, a blockchain platform that launched in 2015 with a cryptocurrency called Ether. Ethereum's founders initially promoted their innovation's similarities to Bitcoin, for understandable reasons, but never progressed to a more mainstream-accessible distinguishing strategy. Most people are aware that Ether is a cryptocurrency like Bitcoin but know little about differences between the two; the familiarizing strategy worked, but Ethereum's distinguishing features (e.g., its ability to verify transactions in a few seconds and its superiority at constructing smart contracts that permit users to exchange things of value, such as shares, property, and money) remained opaque. As a result, the Ether currency—the application Ethereum led with—appeared redundant to many mainstream observers, and Ethereum's use cases were slow to emerge.

3D printing offers another example. When this technology emerged, the name it was given deliberately invoked the concept of printing to help companies understand its basic functionality. As companies became acquainted with 3D printing, they increasingly grasped its versatility and potential and grew eager to try it. At that juncture, the innovation's framing began to highlight its novelty. Increasingly, 3D printing is treated as a subset of additive manufacturing. The term *additive manufacturing* is invoked by inventors at MIT and elsewhere to describe technologies that build 3D objects by iteratively adding material—liquid, powder, sheet material, and so on—layer upon layer. This new designation directs the attention of organizations that never regarded themselves as being in the business of "printing" toward the technology's potential for broader uses, and its supporting ecosystem.[8] This change in framing has been instrumental in the adoption of additive manufacturing technology in industrial and custom manufacturing settings, such as aerospace, automotive, retail, medical, and dental.

The design of e-books' and e-readers' user interfaces exhibits a similar pattern: borrowing a familiar frame to stimulate early adoption, and later introducing novel frames to emphasize the innovation's advantages. When e-readers such as Amazon's Kindle and Barnes & Noble's Nook debuted, their user interfaces emphasized the Next Page button; animation simulated a book page being turned. Both features evoked book reading for the benefit of early users who expected book reading to entail sequential pages. Later iterations differentiated themselves from paper books by adding touchscreens, infinite scrolling, and such now familiar digital actions as tapping on a word to access its definition and tapping on a page to insert a bookmark. Over time, e-readers acquired advanced technology-enhanced tools (highlights, notes, lookup, thesaurus)[9] that traditional books lack, while retaining the basic resemblance that had drawn new customers into the fold.

Transitioning from the Familiar to the Novel

A central question remains: How and when should innovators begin shifting their framing from the familiar to the novel? Our research suggests a two-step approach. First, innovators should begin to describe the technology in more detail once it has gained some initial traction with users. For example, the insurance industry was among the first non-engineering industries to embrace computers. As the industry began using early versions of the computer in the 1950s and 1960s, computer manufacturers gradually began publicly describing the technology as possessing certain brainlike characteristics, such as memory. Gradually, how computer manufacturers promoted computers in public also began to change. It became more common to refer to the computer's ability to think and reason, and its usefulness in compiling information and preparing reports for management and other users. Thus, emphasizing an innovation's novel features eventually enables it to be compared to an analog of what initially appeared unsuitably dissimilar.[10]

Such discourse spread the idea that computer technology could aid in decision-making, which prompted the insurance industry and, later, other industries to rely on computers not just for output, such as processing transactions, but also for sophisticated decision-making. The overall effect is a broadening of the descriptions in the conceptual focus of users. As the use of computers increased over time, the machine analogy weakened, while the brain analogy was more frequently used.[11]

The second step is a mirror image of the first: as the novel aspects are gradually described in more detail, the familiar aspects should be referred to more generically (in less detail). For example, consider the Internet of Things (IoT). To encourage early adoption, innovators framed IoT familiarly as a network of devices capable of sharing data with each other without human intervention; this framing emphasized the centrality of commonly understood phenomena such as networks, devices, computers, machines, and data. Later, to promote broader adoption of IoT, innovators in the technology industry started de-emphasizing familiar frames by replacing previously specific terms used to describe IoT (networks, devices, computers, machines, and data) with more generalized terminology ("anything connected to the internet"). Meanwhile, the same innovators were becoming more specific in their novelty-framed language. For example, the terms "IoT edge computing" or "IoT edge devices" are now increasingly frequently used to get across that computing is happening closer to "the edge"— that is, to the locales where devices and individuals create or use the information in question (versus a central location that might be thousands of miles away). Such increased specificity in language conveys more information—in this case, about the relevance of devices that are not merely connected but connected in a geographically proximate way that helps address challenges of network congestion and latency.[12] It has also familiarized audiences with the breadth of possible applications of connected devices that will not strain the network.

The emergence and evolution of the drone industry appears to be following a similar path. The term *drone* initially associated the technology with a weapon. That familiar frame promoted adoption and use of the new technology, especially by the military. But the uses of drones transcend those of weapons. To emphasize the technology's novelty and broader applications, innovators introduced the term *unmanned aerial vehicles*. They also began using more granular descriptions of specific uses for drones, such as faster and cheaper package delivery, HD filming, and prescription dispatching.[13] This increased descriptive specificity had the effect of reinforcing perceptions of drones as all-purpose tools; that process went hand in hand with an accelerated decrease in describing drones as weapons. As a consequence, military connotations are slowly becoming peripheral in the discourse about drones.

Making familiarity-framed descriptions more generic results in less fervor about qualities that appear redundant with previous technologies; making novelty-framed descriptions more specific underlines the distinctiveness of the new innovation's features and functionality.

Conclusion

How innovators frame new-to-the-world technology shapes its assimilation and adoption (see figure 6.1 for a summary). Theory and practice both suggest that people don't want something truly new; they want familiarity too. But we find that emphasizing the familiar when promoting innovations can have negative consequences for organizations: it makes existing solutions the conceptual focus, rather than the new ones. Consequently, though rendering the unfamiliar more familiar is helpful at the outset, to promote assimilation, it can negatively affect later traction because the new technology's novel aspects get pushed to the periphery. Thus innovators should introduce an innovation by anchoring it in familiarity, and later accentuate its novelty.

One promising way to manage this transition and tension between familiar and novel framing is through the interplay of generalization and specification in descriptions of the technology. Initially, new technology should be described in ways that specify how it aligns with existing technology; such descriptive congruence promotes integration. Later,

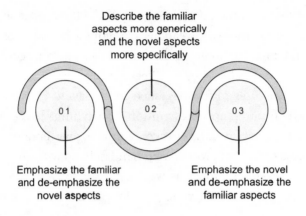

Figure 6.1

as innovators see users beginning to validate the new technology, they should describe it in ways that differentiate it from existing technology with increasing specificity. Doing so will spotlight the key features of the new technology, further clarifying its uniqueness and comparative advantage. In sum, management of change appears to hinge on deftly exploiting the duality of the familiar and the novel (see table 6.1).

Table 6.1
How to frame innovations effectively

Instead of doing this . . .	Do this . . .	And get this result . . .
Framing innovations as *either* familiar *or* novel	Frame innovations as *both* familiar *and* novel.	More success promulgating innovation
Highlighting an innovation's distinctiveness during the earliest stage of adoption	Begin by emphasizing an innovation's similarity to prior solutions; minimize discussion of what is novel.	Increased consumer understanding and use of the new product, system, or process
Continuing to emphasize a new technology's familiar aspects as it takes hold	Shift to emphasizing its novel aspects.	Growing utilization of and demand for the most novel features of the innovation; increasing recognition of its uniqueness and comparative advantage
Making all descriptions of a given innovation either more general or more specific over time	Make descriptions that frame an innovation as familiar more generic over time; make those that frame it as novel more specific over time.	Effective transition from the familiar to the unfamiliar

7 Product versus Purpose: A Productive Tension on the Path to Building Brand Advantage

Google "how to build a brand" and you will be flooded with expert advice: how-to manuals, tips, and steps to building a brand identity that will be memorable, persuasive, and powerful. Meanwhile, managers tend to focus on promoting a brand's quality or on its innovativeness or its environmental friendliness, attributes they think will prove meaningful to customers. But in the pursuit of a strong brand identity, leaders often lose sight of the relationship that matters most. Customers don't typically buy products or services because they're memorable or kind to the environment (These features can help, of course, but they're not persuasive in themselves.) People buy a product or a service to solve a particular problem in their lives. They hire it to do a job. Understanding this relationship when building a brand will result in far more successes than failures.

Understanding the Customer's Job

Customers don't simply buy products or services; they bring them into their lives to make progress on a particular task. In keeping with the insight of Harvard Business School professor Clayton Christensen, we call this progress the *job to be done*, and we say that customers *hire* products or services to perform these jobs.[1] Each job has inherent complexity. It doesn't just have functional dimensions; it has social and emotional dimensions as well.[2] It's not enough to know that a car drives well, for example; it must also be socially and emotionally satisfying to drive. How will you feel when driving the car? Will your co-workers and spouse and kids think it's cool?

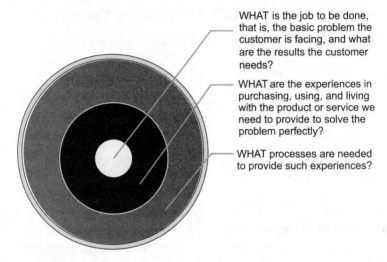

WHAT is the job to be done, that is, the basic problem the customer is facing, and what are the results the customer needs?

WHAT are the experiences in purchasing, using, and living with the product or service we need to provide to solve the problem perfectly?

WHAT processes are needed to provide such experiences?

Figure 7.1

There are three steps involved in creating a product or service that perfectly accomplishes a job to be done: understanding the job, defining the experiences required to do that job, and developing processes to enable these experiences.[3] It's helpful to visualize them as successive questions in a hierarchy, as illustrated in figure 7.1.

1. Understand the Job to be Done   Every job has functional, social, and emotional dimensions whose relative importance varies with the context. Though the products and services that people hire to do specific jobs may change over time, the jobs themselves remain relatively stable. For example, many people want to feel connected with loved ones when they live far away. At one point, most Americans relied on the US Postal Service to do this job; later they may have turned to AT&T. Now they might hire Apple FaceTime or even Facebook Portal for the same purpose, but the underlying job has not changed. Solving customers' problems requires seeing things from their point of view and having deep empathy for their experiences. Senior leaders at IKEA understand, for example, that people who are moving—parents of college-age children, say, or young professionals pursuing career opportunities—usually need at least a few new furnishings straightaway. Sourcing items individually from Craigslist, or waiting months for made-to-order items from West Elm, are less than satisfactory ways to tackle their job to be done.

2. Define the Necessary Purchase and Use Experiences It's essential to know what experiences are needed for a given product to perfectly nail a job. IKEA recognizes that when people want to furnish their homes quickly, they don't want to make multiple trips. They want to bring items home the same day and set up everything with minimal fuss. That's why IKEA provides a one-stop shop where customers can buy everything they need for every room in their house. IKEA also offers same-day delivery services and products that are relatively easy to assemble with a single tool. Ultimately, these experiences, more than a certain set of product features, are the hiring criteria that consumers use to weigh alternatives and select a particular organization's offering to perform the job to be done. In this sense, physical products can be thought of as services. Ask, Do the accompanying experiences help customers make the progress they want to make?

3. Develop Processes to Provide These Experiences Leaders need to rethink and redesign organizational structures to reliably provide these experiences. Doing so will have an impact on such internal and external processes as retail strategy, customer relations, inventory management, and talent acquisition. The goal is to integrate around the experiences needed to get the job done. IKEA adopted a big-box retail format to stock large amounts of inventory and to showcase furnishings for an entire home. Many locations also include on-site dining and day care, reinforcing the company's status as a one-stop shop. Flat-pack furniture ensures that most items can be easily carted home in most vehicles.

The Link to Brands and Their Purpose

Most leaders of innovation distinguish branding and marketing from product development, but we propose an integrated view. The three steps necessary to nail a job to be done lay the foundation for the brand-building process.

As marketing gurus Erich Joachimsthaler and David A. Aaker noted twenty-five years ago, "Advertising has long been the cornerstone of most brand building efforts."[4] Indeed, advertising has conventionally been crucial to brand building, the first step and a repeated step toward success. But we propose that the most valuable possible advertising is a product that performs a job well and does so repeatedly. Organizations that build such products find they need to spend very little on media. Purpose-brand builders view advertising as the last step in the process rather than the first. Its task isn't to raise broad awareness, it's to tie the product ever more closely to the specific job it's designed to do. A prime example is Federal Express, whose classic slogan, "When it absolutely, positively has to be there overnight," inextricably linked the company with reliable overnight delivery.

A *purpose brand* is a brand that is inextricably linked to a particular job to be done, becoming virtually synonymous with the job in prospective customers' minds.[5] It can even prevent a prospective customer from considering other options. A brand that consistently creates the right experiences to perform customers' jobs should say to the customer, in effect, "I understand what you've been looking for. Your search is over." Some purpose brands—Google, Zoom, and Venmo—have become so strongly associated with a particular job that they've become verbs: "Google it." "Let's Zoom." "Venmo me." (Did you notice the first word in this chapter?) Other purpose brands' names conjure up the job they aim to get done. Residence Inn by Marriott suggests a longer stay than is typical at an ordinary hotel, which is exactly the job the chain wants to do for its guests. Airbnb combines "airbed" (the founders' minimalist solution for hosting their first guests) and "bed and breakfast" (an intimate accommodation). The name itself—though it need not do so—can help link the brand to its purpose in prospective customers' minds.

Consider as an example a well-known purpose brand. Someone who needs to file taxes quickly or who has no clue how to prepare them might thank Scott Cook's company Intuit for creating TurboTax software. TurboTax is a purpose brand for a single job: "Help me file my taxes quickly, easily, and as seamlessly as possible." Intuit executives appear to have understood the functional, social, and emotional complexities of handling one's finances thoroughly enough to provide a tailored set of experiences, including real-time chat, audit risk analysis, and constant technical support, that tells customers, "We understand what you're going through." Intuit takes an integrated approach to nailing the job further: by partnering with employers, Intuit automatically imports W-2s into TurboTax, eliminating the friction and annoyance of manual entry.

A well-designed purpose brand functions like a compass for both customers and company staff. It guides customers to the products that will do the job they need done.[6] Indeed, a purpose brand centered over a compelling job is often able to command a premium price for providing this service. A purpose brand also guides the organization's product designers and marketers as they develop new and improved offerings, helping them make apt choices about which features, experiences, and functions are relevant to the job. It helps them decide which features to improve and which to leave alone. In essence, the brand creates its own roadmap for the future—an invaluable asset for startups (in fact, for all organizations) where what *not* to do is often a fraught question. An effective purpose brand helps leaders see which organizational processes are necessary and which are not, as the organization maps its "what's next" strategy.

You can see this roadmap at work at GOJO Industries, the inventors of Purell hand sanitizer.[7] GOJO got its start after World War II. During the war, Goldie Lippman worked at a rubber plant in Akron, Ohio. She wanted a product to clean her hands that was safer than the harsh chemicals being used. Her husband, Jerry, with the help of a local professor, found an answer. They called their new product GOJO Hand Cleaner. Goldie managed purchasing and bookkeeping, while Jerry sold the product from the back of his car. But customers objected that the product was too expensive, and Jerry soon figured out why: employees were scooping more cleaner from the jars than they needed and were even taking it home. And so Jerry invented (and patented) the first portion-controlled hand-cleaner dispenser.

Over the years, as the company expanded into new locations, GOJO marketers realized that customers didn't necessarily need to remove heavy dirt; they often just wanted to quickly sanitize their hands. That realization gave rise to Purell, invented in 1988 and first marketed to consumers in 1997. Since then, it has led to such improvements as touch-free and counter-mounted dispensing systems and to new products, such as Purell Surface Spray. These products played a crucial role in protecting people during the COVID-19 pandemic. The entire organization was built on a single job, and its many products all evolved from that one job it had nailed perfectly.

A purpose brand's firm link to a job to be done creates enormous opportunities for differentiation, premium pricing, and growth. For instance, some of the biggest successes in consumer-packaged goods in recent years have not been flashy new products but unusual uses of long-established products.[8] Abbott Laboratories' Pedialyte is a good example: the electrolyte-laden fluid had been marketed since the 1960s as a dehydration remedy for sick babies and toddlers, but adults had begun using it after a bout of stomach flu or, more unexpectedly, to nullify a hangover's effects.[9] Abbott took to targeting partygoers through a newly energized social media effort and distribution of the product at music festivals and sporting events.[10] Launched just prior to New Year's Eve in 2018, Pedialyte Sparkling Rush powder packs promised "a fizzy way to quickly replenish fluids and electrolytes lost to dehydration."[11] Adults now consume one in every three bottles sold.[12]

Building a Purpose Brand: Under Armour

The story of Under Armour exemplifies of how a purpose brand, if well designed around a clear job to be done, can sell itself.[13] From the start the company's founder, Kevin Plank, had understood the job his sportswear needed to do, and the experiences it should provide. In 1992, despite his small stature, Plank made the University of Maryland's football team on the strength of a tryout (rather than recruitment).[14] Through hard work, he became a starting fullback and eventually the special team's captain.[15] Meanwhile, Plank thought a lot about how to improve his performance. He soon realized that his uniform wasn't helping.

Plank sweated a lot; he described himself as the "sweatiest player on the field."[16] The uniform's cotton base layer made matters worse. It got wet and bunched up under the bulky plastic shoulder pads. "I saw those soaking-wet heavy T-shirts," Plank recalls, "and I thought, 'This is just crazy, because when I take this thing off and it hits the floor, it makes this big *suuup* sound. There *has* to be something better.'"[17] A dry shirt weighed only about six ounces. Add sweat and it could weigh up to three pounds. The shirt was literally slowing players down. "It wasn't just uncomfortable—I really believed the extra weight hurt an athlete's performance," he says.

Plank's own experience equipped him to understand what others must be experiencing and to more effectively nail this job: "As an athlete, I had a direct understanding of what it meant to be a football player, and that feeling of standing there with athletes that look bigger and faster and stronger than me, and wondering: beyond physical capabilities, what else could I utilize to help give me some version of an advantage? That's when I had the idea."[18]

The stretchy garment under his uniform pants, which secured his thigh pads, always stayed dry during practice. Why couldn't a similar fabric be used for undershirts?[19] Plank visited fabric wholesalers in New York's garment district and experimented with various kinds of nylon and polyester developed for the lingerie industry.[20] He learned that polyester, which repels water, could be modified with a silicone-based solution to draw moisture away from the skin and then release it (a property called "wicking").[21] Adding spandex fiber to the fabric caused it to cling tightly to the wearer's body and compress the muscles—a feature believed to improve endurance and speed recovery.[22] After graduating in 1996, Plank made a prototype base layer for football players and began selling the product from his grandmother's basement.[23]

His early sales efforts promoted the experience the product provided. Plank sent his shirts to friends at college and in National Football League (NFL) programs, along with forms for ordering more.[24] "I tried to emphasize that an Under Armour shirt could help these athletes improve their performance. I positioned wearing it as a tool to help them, rather than a favor to me."[25] Early adopters of the distinctive form-fitting shirts were initially mocked: "What the heck are you wearing? Is that a *bro*-ssiere?," Plank recalled a player saying. But as the benefits of comfort and enhanced performance became clear, more and more athletes gave it a try.

Plank and his team focused relentlessly on overcoming obstacles and enhancing performance. Indeed, athletes reported feeling euphoric when wearing the product. They *felt* like they were performing better; the product boosted their confidence.[26] By nailing this job, the purpose brand seemed to sell itself. Under Armour made its first major sale to the Georgia Tech football team in 1997. After Georgia Tech played Clemson and Florida State, both schools also placed orders.[27] Teams' equipment managers were instrumental: Plank discovered that they communicated regularly among themselves and in many cases were authorized to make teamwide purchases.[28] The Atlanta Falcons of the NFL placed an order following a conversation between their equipment manager and the staff at Georgia Tech; after playing the Falcons, the New York Giants also called Under Armour. "It was really one athlete to another, one step at a time," Plank marvels. "Next thing you know, one guy turns into two guys, turns into the whole side of a locker room, and then the whole team. And then one team plays another."[29]

Success outstripped Plank's original ambitions. Initially, he recalled, "I just wanted to make the world's greatest T-shirt for football players. If I solve that problem, I'm going to do fine." But the product's versatility soon became evident: "The football players that we sold it to also played baseball; they also played lacrosse. And then they had girlfriends that played lacrosse and soccer and field hockey, and one by one I realized the demand for our base layer was much bigger."[30] Soon kids began wearing their football base layer turtlenecks under their parkas when they went snowboarding. Then military personnel began placing orders. Eventually the products, which by then included an expanded garment line, were popular with weekend warriors on and off the field.

Under Armour remained steadfastly focused on developing products that improved athletic performance. Publicity came cheap, if not free. *USA Today* ran a front-page photo of an athlete wearing an Under Armour turtleneck. When Plank heard about the filming of a new football movie, *Any Given Sunday*, he reached out to its director, Oliver Stone. Stone admired Under Armour's grassroots NFL appeal and requested apparel for the whole cast. Despite the film's huge promotional value, Plank billed Stone.[31] Indeed, early on, the company took a stand against providing free apparel for endorsements and product placements. When the Miami Dolphins requested free shirts for the team in 1997, Under Armour refused. The company also rejected baseball star Barry Bonds's $5,000 asking price to be photographed in Under Armour apparel in 1998. Ultimately the Dolphins paid, and Bonds did the shoot in exchange for some Under Armour gear.[32] Plank's view was that the product had to be "more compelling than what you had to *pay* someone to wear!"[33]

When the company did pay for ads, they underscored the product's ultimate job: helping athletes improve their performance. Under Armour's first TV advertising campaign, "Protect this House," appeared in 2003. It featured montages of workouts in weight rooms and on practice fields. In the ad, an anonymous player, a college teammate of Plank's, led a passionate team chant: "Will you protect this house? I will!" The slogan's focus on teamwork and preparation resonated with athletes and fans across the country, and was invoked by sports anchors and TV personalities like David Letterman.[34] By 2005, Under Armour had reached $281.1 million in sales and $35.8 million in net income. After twenty years of growth unprecedented in the industry, the company's global sales came to exceed $5 billion. The former upstart had also successfully broken into the athletic apparel and footwear market, dominated by Nike and Adidas. It's a textbook case of purpose-brand building (see figure 7.2).

Under Armour seems to have stalled in recent years (a development we alluded to in the opening chapter of the book). We'll explain how leaders' handling of the product-versus-purpose tension is implicated in these recent struggles.

The Challenge of Extending a Purpose Brand to New Products

To expand, leaders can introduce a new product under the umbrella of an existing brand that logically extends that brand. This involves

Performance-enhancing, comfortable, moisture-wicking undergarments for athletes

Affordable, effective, reliable, lightweight, and procurable through a multitude of channels

Customer testing across multiple different types of activities; comparative advantage over competitors. Furthering market success outside college athletes (military, golfing, etc.).

Figure 7.2
Building a purpose brand at Under Armour.

creating a two-tier brand architecture: the original brand becomes, in effect, an endorser lending legitimacy to the new product. For example, Crest toothpaste, a P&G brand associated with clean, healthy teeth, became the endorser brand for White Strips, a product developed to address the specific job of "Help me whiten my teeth." The concept of a two-tier brand architecture raises a fundamental question about purpose brands: How far can they be extended? Does the endorser concept imply that there is no limit to the number of new products a company can introduce?

Brand extension is a controversial issue in marketing. Some experts argue that practically all extensions are mistakes, that a brand should maintain a narrow focus.[35] Others look at the enormous cost of launching a new brand—estimates run from $50 million to well over $100 million[36]—and think it makes sense to leverage an already successful brand. Doing so worked out well for Diet Coke and the iPhone. Leaders of innovation usually occupy the middle ground: they appreciate the potential of brand extension but see the risks of undermining the original brand.

Research has generated some rules that leaders can follow to capitalize on purpose-brand extensions while minimizing risks:[37]

- *Do* extend the brand to new products that can be hired to do the *same job*; doing so will not muddle what the brand stands for. Sony was able to extend its Walkman brand from the original product, a portable tape player, to a new product, a portable CD player, because, in that pre-MP3 era, the fundamental job was the same: playing recorded music while on the go.

- *Don't* extend the original purpose brand to target other jobs; the brand could lose its meaning to consumers and become diluted. Different jobs demand different purpose brands. For example, when Ford purchased the Volvo brand in 1999, it created flashier cars to compete with luxury vehicles like BMW and Mercedes; safety was downplayed in its marketing. The result was not merely a decline in sales but also an opening in the market for competitors to tout their own cars' safety features—Volvo no longer owned that status. By 2005 the company was no longer profitable, and in 2010 Ford gave up on it altogether, selling it at a substantial loss to the Chinese carmaker Geely.[38] "We lost our way," Volvo North America CEO Tony Nicolosi told *Autoweek* in 2013. "We gotta go back to our roots. Society is coming back to what we represent as a brand: environment, family, safety. We've just been poor at communicating it."[39]

- Leaders *can* use an existing brand to endorse a product that does a different job, but need to take an extra step to *create a new purpose brand* for the product in question. Such "sub-brands," as they are often called, will not harm the original brand as long as they fulfill their own purpose. And they will benefit from the legitimacy of the endorser brand. For example, Marriott created the Residence Inn and Executive Apartments brands of extended-stay suites to perform a specific set of jobs related to temporary housing. Compared with the company's flagship Marriott Hotels & Resorts properties, Residence Inn by Marriott rooms feature full kitchens, comfortable seating areas, social programming, and grocery delivery.

- *Use two-word brand architecture* to distinguish the endorser brand (Marriott) from the newly created purpose brand (Courtyard). This is an especially important step when moving down-market to tap into disruptive growth opportunities. We have seen this phenomenon play out with UberPool and UberEats.

Pitfalls and Challenges

Purpose brands are rare. Given their success rate, we might ask why this is the case.

One explanation could be that marketers are unwilling to do the hard work required to identify specific jobs to be done. Everybody knows why people buy cars or soda; who needs research? If they do undertake market research, marketers are likely to rely on the kind of segmentation afforded by demographic or psychographic data. But jobs to be done rarely line up neatly with customary segmentation categories, such as gender, age, and income levels. Moreover, these jobs are often unexpected. There is no substitute for observing and talking to potential customers and then assembling the resulting information into a coherent picture of the progress those customers are trying to make in their lives.

But the primary reason for the scarcity of purpose brands may be inherent in the tensions of building one. A purpose brand is designed to do one particular job. Its marketers naturally focus on the connection between the brand and that job. What they don't want to do is to suggest that the product might also do lots of *other* jobs. Thus they are in effect deliberately excluding numerous potential customers. Such exclusiveness can be terrifying to a corporate executive or an aspiring entrepreneur; the temptation to expand into other areas is both structural and hard to resist. Successful brands tend to accumulate precisely the kind of ambition, capital, and organizational capacity that make expanding into adjacent product categories possible. Over time, a blossoming purpose brand will be presented with plenty of potentially lucrative opportunities to enter new markets. With investors always hungry for growth, it takes guts and brand discipline to say no. Doing so is essential to purpose branding.[40]

Even as Under Armour's apparel line was growing in popularity and spreading organically across the athletic and fitness markets, the company's leaders were reluctant to extend the brand beyond what they saw as their core market. Shoes and cleats were a logical extension, but high-fashion athleisurewear was out (for the time being; they would later revisit the idea). Under Armour was also approached about a cobranded sports drink (pass) and workwear for construction and medical applications. Doctors, nurses, physical therapists, and other medical personnel who had some leeway about what they wore to work needed high-performance fabrics that could stand up to long active days on the job. The boxy, heavyweight cotton scrubs worn by these professionals in clinics and operating rooms around the world seemed ripe for upgrading. But Under Armour passed, reasoning that the target customer might not align with its strategy at the time of being the go-to brand for functional athletic apparel. "We probably would have made a lot of money, but it wasn't right for a sports brand," a senior executive explained. "It didn't fit."[41]

But as the cases of other sports apparel companies missing the emergence of the base layer market remind us, one brand's pass can become a new brand's purpose. FIGS, a brand of fashion-forward scrubs founded in 2013 by a former medical student, Heather Hasson, who had hand-altered her own scrubs for a better fit, saw the same opportunity and ran with it.[42] The FIGS origin story, like Under Armour's, features an innovator solving a specific need with a bootstrapped solution. While selling the makeshift products out of the trunks of their cars, with the parking lot of Cedars Sinai Medical Center in Los Angeles playing the same role as the University of Maryland locker room, Hasson and cofounder Trina Spear realized they had tapped into market demand that existing players had simply overlooked. FIGS has since built a strong purpose brand as the comfortable and fashionable wear-to-work alternative for the medical community.

Focus has to be maintained at length or the distinctiveness of a purpose brand will dissipate into thin air. Take the example of the Mini. Originally a British marque built on the distinctive small-car styling popular in Europe, the brand was acquired by BMW in the 1990s and reintroduced to North American audiences with a major marketing push in the early 2000s. Extensive brand marketing during those years included prominent placements in the third *Austin Powers* movie and a remake of *The Italian Job*, both of which showcased the car's distinctive size and sporty look in photogenic European locales. The meaning of the Mini brand, both historically and during its early BMW years, was clear: small, sporty, and distinctly European.

Sales grew steadily throughout the early 2000s, though Mini remained something of a niche brand. In 2011, amid slumping sales and visions of growth in the lucrative small SUV market, Mini introduced its Mini Countryman SUV. Designers were careful to maintain the distinctive Mini styling, but critics questioned the move. "At the risk of being puritanical, it seems to me that sometimes car companies have to walk away from the short-term expedience of a few thousand sales, or even a few tens of thousands of sales, to protect the meaning, the truth, the inner logic of a brand," wrote Dan Neil in the *Wall Street Journal*. "Mini has spent years selling itself as automotive counterprogramming, and now it's acting like every other car maker with white space to fill."[43] The gambit appeared to work at first—sales jumped in 2011 and 2012— but Mini's sales have steadily declined since their 2012 peak,[44] leading some to question whether the move to serve new markets had unraveled the focused magic of the Mini brand.[45]

Focus is scary, until leaders realize that it merely means turning their backs on markets they could never have served well anyway. An unwavering focus on the jobs that customers are trying to accomplish promises greatly improved odds of success in new-product development and brand building.

Conclusion

Building a successful purpose brand is every marketer's dream. Well-designed purpose brands can sell themselves, enable premium pricing, and lock out competitors. But history shows that failures are far more common than successes. Why? Largely because leaders focus too much on brand identity and image when they should be thinking about perfecting and supporting a brand's purpose: helping customers do a job, which is more important to customers (see table 7.1). We recommend that leaders integrate branding and marketing with product development and take these three steps: (1) learn how a brand can meet customers' functional, emotional, and social needs; (2) ensure that customers' experiences when purchasing and using the product nail the job perfectly; and (3) develop and align processes to intensify these experiences if a brand is to truly become synonymous with the job to be done. Once a purpose brand gains traction, it's time to figure out whether to take yet another step: using the purpose brand to endorse and legitimize other brands.

Table 7.1
Building and extending a purpose brand

Instead of doing this . . .	Do this . . .	And get this result . . .
Overly focusing on brand identity and image	Think harder about perfecting a brand's purpose: helping address the job to be done, the basic problem customers are facing and the solution they crave.	Valuable products and services that customers are willing to bring into their lives to make progress on a particular task
Looking for jobs to be done using traditional market research or segmentation categories, such as gender, age, and income levels	Watch what customers do, and get explanations for what people hired instead.	A coherent picture of the progress those customers are trying to make in their lives
Assuming that customers make purchasing decisions on the basis of a certain set of product features	Find out what collateral experiences (social, emotional, functional, etc.) should accompany a product to perfectly nail a job to be done.	Enormous opportunities for differentiation, premium pricing, and growth
Spending money lavishly early on for advertising, marketing, and media	Design organizational structures to reliably provide the experiences that customers crave.	A roadmap for the future
Extending the brand to target jobs far afield from its purpose	Extend the brand to *new products* that can be hired to do *the same job.*	No loss of the brand's meaning to consumers and no dilution
Standing pat with the existing brand	Use the existing brand to endorse the quality of a product that does a different job, then create a new purpose brand around that product.	New-brand benefits attributable to the legitimacy of the endorser brand

8 When It's Time to Pivot, What's Your Story? How to Sell Stakeholders on a New Strategy

In 1908 Roald Amundsen of Norway planned an expedition to the North Pole. He convinced scientists to share their expertise and equipment, won a grant from the Norwegian parliament, and persuaded other backers to pour money into the project. Amundsen borrowed the four hundred-ton three-masted schooner *Fram* and recruited men willing to risk their lives on a journey through the icy Bering Strait. Ordinary Norwegians cheered him on, imagining that he would plant their flag in a land where no one had ever been. But just before setting sail, Amundsen got word that the Americans Robert Peary and Frederick Cook had beaten him to the North Pole.[1] Now what?

Amundsen's quandary is all too familiar to innovators. Launching an ambitious endeavor requires enormous support. You need funding and staff. You need media coverage to build credibility. To attract all those resources, you need a good story. The story usually focuses on a problem and a solution, a plan and a goal, and it usually features the talents of the leadership team. It's told with passion and conviction. With any luck, enthusiasm builds around the story and resources flow in, along with employees and new partners and, eventually, customers. But often leaders realize during this process that they've made a mistake—that the plan was wrong, that they've cajoled people to invest time and money and effort in something that won't work. They need to pivot.[2]

Changing direction is, in theory, a good thing for a business or a new initiative. The path to enduring success is rarely a straight line. Cornelius Vanderbilt switched from steamships to railroads, William Wrigley from baking powder to chewing gum. Twitter launched as a podcast directory, Yelp began as an automated email service, and You-Tube was once a dating site. Leaders who reinvent their businesses—deliberately becoming a different kind of organization (not jumping aimlessly from one failed venture to another)—shrink their chances of failure by conserving resources while continuing to learn more about customers, business partners, and new technologies.[3]

But pivots can incur a penalty if they're not correctly managed. A reorientation is an implicit admission that the plan to which leaders were once deeply committed was flawed. This deviation can be jarring, and can suggest a lack of consistency and competence. Resource providers, employees, journalists, and customers all require a coherent explanation of why things went wrong and what will happen next. They need to be persuaded to stick around.

Like scientists, leaders of innovation generate and test hypotheses to find viable solutions; that's the basis of the lean startup approach to launching companies.[4] But the same leaders must also be as adept as politicians at convincingly justifying shifts in position and managing diverse audiences along the way. This blend of skills became even more important during the upheaval caused by COVID-19. Many businesses that were experiencing high growth rates until the pandemic saw revenues fall and scrambled to devise new business models and to reformulate their strategies. Some new business ventures found tremendous opportunities in the early phases of the crisis, such as by servicing the stay-at-home economy, only to see those opportunities disappear when social distancing eased. The long-term impact on consumer behavior is still anyone's guess. The companies most likely to endure will be those that can adapt nimbly—and bring stakeholders along with them.

How can leaders do this? Jointly with our research colleagues, we conducted ninety interviews with founders, corporate innovation chiefs, market analysts, and financial journalists. We also reviewed dozens of press releases, analysts' reports, and media stories of both high- and low-performing companies, many in new technology sectors.[5] In the course of this research, we identified stratagems that are critical to securing and maintaining stakeholders' support during major reboots. We've come

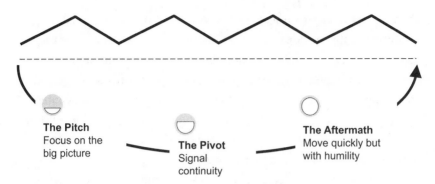

Figure 8.1

to view the need to sell a pivot as a productive tension that gives rise to such stratagems. This chapter lays out the process—the sequence of steps—by which leaders can maintain *consistency* in their organizations amid inevitable adaptation and change (see figure 8.1 for a preview).

The Pitch: Focus on the Big Picture

To build early credibility, particularly with resource providers and partners, leaders must create a unique, concrete plan that meets a specific market need or solves a specific problem. It should include a well-formed product concept and a path to growth and profitability. Yet in their eagerness to gain initial support for their solutions, leaders often box themselves into a corner: The more specific a narrative is, the more likely it is to turn out to be wrong. To avoid this trap, our research shows, savvy leaders craft broad narratives—umbrella ambitions rather than narrow solutions—that leave room to maneuver.

Doing so requires resisting the urge to be precise about features or functionality, particularly early on. Like effective political leaders, effective leaders of innovation communicate by means of emotional appeals and underscore a larger aim. They don't lay out a roadmap; they promise to reach a destination. Microsoft is modernizing the workspace. LinkedIn is connecting the world's professionals to make them more productive and successful. Patagonia is in business to save the planet. This doesn't mean that leaders abandon credibility or resign themselves to being undisciplined. In fact, wielding big abstract ideas encourages audiences to see what they want to see—much as, according to political science research, voters respond positively to candidates whose ambiguous statements on issues leave their views open to interpretation (which can later help them avoid charges of flip-flopping).[6] Our research indicates that leaders of innovation who take a similar approach with stakeholders generate more enthusiasm and support, and ultimately win more resources and traction.

Our business school colleagues often scold companies for vision statements that are vague or filled with platitudes. But emphasizing widely accepted principles, particularly popular ones, can be useful when seeking to sell stakeholders on an early-stage pivot. Consider the early days of Netflix. Founder Reed Hastings, anticipating a later switch to streaming video, began with the stated purpose of offering the best home video viewing for everyone—not offering DVDs by mail, which was the company's actual product. As the organization pivoted to digital distribution, the original sweeping formulation still made sense. Even the company's name supported its future course. Hastings said he had wanted to be ready for video on demand when the technology permitted, and that's why he had called the company Netflix.[7]

But to satisfy backers' demand for precision and differentiation in pitches, innovators risk spelling out who they are and what they are doing too early and too explicitly, before either is entirely clear. Then, when they change course, they run into image problems by appearing to be inconsistent, insincere, or overly opportunistic. Magic Leap, a pioneer in augmented reality (AR), is a good example. Pitching its nascent product as a high-quality gaming headset for consumers, the company carefully crafted a whimsical image with slogans like "Free Your Mind" and "Enter the Magicverse." But when uptake of AR by game developers and consumers was slower than expected, the firm's executives began looking to other markets, bidding on a government contract to sell AR headsets to the army. Magic Leap didn't win the contract, and in a column published by Quartz, it was ridiculed for trying to pivot from "delightful consumer tech" to "lethal military gear."[8]

The Pivot: Signal Continuity

The human mind values consistency. Our analysis of media coverage of companies, and of feedback from customers, partners, and investors, shows that audiences are thrown by a confusing plot; they view inconsistent organizations as less legitimate and ultimately less deserving of their support. But they're also less likely to register a deviation as significant if it seems to be in line with previously articulated larger aims. The link between the new strategic direction and the initial pitch isn't always obvious, however; to maintain credibility and avoid being penalized, leaders need to make the connection explicit.

When Steph Korey and Jen Rubio, cofounders of the luggage startup Away, realized that their first suitcases wouldn't be ready for Christmas (as they'd promised investors, customers, journalists, and other stakeholders), they threw themselves into producing a coffee table book about travel that would be packaged with a gift card redeemable for a bag the next year. The move looked like a radical departure from their plan, and could easily have caused unnerved supporters to abandon the young venture. Yet the founders maintained credibility and support by spelling out how the move jibed with their higher-level goal: building a travel and lifestyle brand. Luggage was a key part of that brand, but a book worked too. Investors were convinced; so were journalists. A number of media outlets ran holiday gift–buying features about a suitcase that didn't yet exist. Within a few weeks, two thousand books had been sold (meaning that two thousand bags had been pre-ordered), and the founders requested a second print run.[9]

A linking tactic of that sort works even better if the enterprise's overriding aim matches a larger societal objective. In fact, research suggests that people pursuing meaningful missions are less bothered by course corrections along the way.[10] Two companies we studied in depth illustrate this point. Both began by offering a niche service that enabled members of an online community to duplicate the financial transactions of skilled investors. The idea was to attract talented investors to the sites, identify the best among them, and leverage their investment strategies. The companies launched within six months of each other, with similar amounts of funding and teams with roughly similar credentials. Eventually both abandoned the initial concept and pivoted to become automated software-based investing services. Yet one became the leader in the nascent automated investment advisory sector, with more than $1 billion under management, while the other was forced to sell off its assets and shut down. After conducting an in-depth comparative analysis, we concluded that a key explanation for their divergent trajectories boiled down to how the two companies had handled their stakeholders. The successful company never wavered from its overriding mission to "democratize finance" even as it shifted strategies. The CEO positioned the changed business plan as just another way to meet the same goal to which stakeholders were committed.

The unsuccessful company, on the other hand, reframed each new business iteration by adopting a new goal, from "Bring transparency to investing information" to "Make investing social" to creating a "Trusted investment advisory." Worse—unlike his counterpart, who warned stakeholders of imminent changes—the CEO and his team barely communicated with affected stakeholders, sowing further doubt that the transitions were wise. After his company's demise, the CEO pointed to messaging whiplash as a key reason for the company's inability to keep stakeholders on board. "After you pivot, your new positioning can be confusing to customers and partners who paid attention to your original PR," he explained.

Pivoting away from an overly specific initial pitch is difficult, but it's not impossible to save face and retain stakeholder confidence. The key is to revisit and broaden—not change—the original pitch. Consider 3D Robotics (3DR). In the early 2010s, it was a rapidly growing consumer drone company with over three hundred fifty employees and nearly $100 million in funding from Qualcomm Ventures, Richard Branson, and others. But by 2015, 3DR was being hammered by competitors that offered better and cheaper drones. Worse, unforeseen manufacturing issues forced the company to delay the launch of a flagship drone; then, when it finally arrived, it was plagued by technical flaws. Holiday sales suffered, money was running out, and employees began leaving. Everyone was rattled, especially investors.[11]

In a last-ditch effort to keep the company alive, CEO Chris Anderson, a former editor-in-chief of *Wired*, orchestrated a major pivot to drone software and services for enterprises. Initially, this sudden change in narrative was disconcerting. Some media outlets deemed the company a total failure. Anderson himself acknowledged that he'd grossly underestimated the competition. Nonetheless, Anderson managed to calm investors by skillfully communicating a sense of continuity. How? In essence, he revisited and broadened the original pitch to encompass enterprise software: 3DR was about extending the internet to the sky. Whether it was doing so for consumers or for businesses, using drones or some other method, was beside the point. Some investors bought the revised pitch. Despite 3DR's rocky past, the company managed to secure another $80 million in funding to support the new direction. The tactic of revisiting and broadening the pitch is not without risk. It is rarely feasible to recast everything leaders end up doing as part of the original strategy, and no leader wants to be seen as gaslighting stakeholders. Crafting a broad narrative early on, we've learned, is a more robust approach.

When managing pivots, the stakes are even higher than for new ventures. Legacy processes and structures—those that helped the organization succeed in the past—become a liability but are extremely difficult to change. Sometimes mass layoffs are inevitable. Morale suffers. And these companies are often punished by financial markets, as the general public scrutinizes their tough but necessary decisions. Again, a key to success is having crafted a narrative that is sufficiently broad and then explicitly linking a pivot to the initial pitch. Salesforce is an example of a large organization that does this well. Salesforce contextualizes each new product release within its larger, more meaningful aim of "democratizing digital transformation." Step one, check. Step two, then, is linking a strategic change to that broad mission. Salesforce did just that with its 2017 launch of Einstein Analytics, a data analysis tool powered by artificial intelligence (AI), and subsequent introductions of new Einstein services.[12] All of these actions were justified as contributions to the company's efforts to "democratize AI development." Press releases, interviews, and marketing materials all invoke the same refrain—giving small businesses access to the same technologies as large companies—thus making all forays into new territory seem consistent with larger ambitions.

The Aftermath: Move Quickly but with Humility

Leaders of innovation must move fast to capture fleeting opportunities. Resource restraints and time constraints often preclude more measured approaches, such as a phased withdrawal from a legacy product or market. But swift retreats don't always sit well with existing customers and other stakeholders, who may feel abandoned after a major reboot.

Empathy and remorse are a balm when informing people of changes they may not welcome. Stakeholders (especially employees and early customers, who are most at risk of alienation) are far more willing to remain loyal if they're given guidance about how they'll be affected by a change, and if leaders seem to genuinely care about their situation. "Act with common decency" may seem like unnecessary advice, but it's worth being reminded.

Too many leaders consider empathy a sign of weakness, or fear that stakeholders will lose faith if they apologize for a pivot. Terrified of losing support—and committed to the uncompromising efficiency logic of lean startups—some leaders simply make the change and never admit they were wrong. Instead of preparing audiences for a change, they spring it on them. Only when stakeholders react—sometimes harshly—do they apologize. By then it's too late, and they're on the defensive.

As an example of the issues created by a poorly managed strategic transition, consider Tesla. In 2019, Elon Musk decided to shutter most of Tesla's retail stores for electric vehicles. He had concluded that car prices had to be cut to stimulate demand, sales had to move online, and staff had to be let go. Without informing employees, customers, the conventional media, or Wall Street first, Musk released the news—but buried the announcement about closures and layoffs in a boosterish email to employees about new car models, pricing issues, and new investments in service and manufacturing. CNBC published a copy of the email; Tesla then released it publicly. The media attacked the company, its pricing model, and its constantly changing strategy. Ten days later, Musk backpedaled. Tesla would keep "significantly more" stores open than previously announced. He offered little explanation for why the change of plans. But by then it didn't matter. Musk—who almost always owns the narrative—had lost control of this one. Journalists quickly pounced on the new story, questioning the competency of Tesla's leadership and speculating about whether stronger middle management was required, and whether Tesla employees would even stick around.[13] All of this could have been avoided, we suspect, by staging the transition more carefully, keeping stakeholders informed, and showing some empathy.

Netflix provides another example of what not to do. Trouble began in 2011, when Netflix surprised customers with a 60 percent price hike and an announcement that the company would start charging separately for its streaming video and DVD services.[14] The unwelcome news was accompanied by little information about how people would be affected, both confusing and infuriating customers. Then CEO Reed Hastings made matters worse: a blog post apologizing for the price hike mentioned in passing that the company would split off DVD-by-mail into a separate business called Qwikster. This announcement too caught audiences off-guard, and the backlash from customers, media, and investors intensified. Thousands of consumers and commentators replied to Hastings's blog, calling him arrogant and criticizing the plan. Hastings followed up with an announcement that Netflix would abandon plans for a split altogether. The series of stumbles caused shares to tumble 77 percent during the period, undermined stakeholders' faith in Hastings and the company, and illustrated how not to handle audiences during big transitions. When asked later how he might have done things differently, Hastings praised proactive communication: people who are treated sincerely, he said, can handle even terrible news.

Compare these examples with how Glitch's transformation into Slack was handled. In 2012, Glitch was a struggling online collaborative

video game. Then its leaders, having realized that the messaging technology they'd developed to enable gamers to communicate with each
other would make a terrific tool for companies, transitioned to that
more promising business.[15] Glitch's leaders expressed humility and
regret for how others would be affected: in plain if somewhat sappy
language, the company issued an apology, explaining that the game
had failed to attract enough players.[16] It empathized with those who
had signed up, thanked them for their support, and provided useful
information about the shutdown, such as refund details. The leadership mentioned the new messaging product in passing but concentrated on articulating concern for employees who would lose their jobs.
The message to stakeholders was honest, helpful, and sensitive to their
needs. In short, it was kind. The company announced the decision and
moved on. In the end, Glitch's transformation didn't provoke a serious backlash—a big risk, especially when tech users feel spurned—and
the new business launched with roughly $17 million in funding from
Accel Partners and Andreessen Horowitz, both original Glitch investors. At the time of its pivot, Glitch had some committed users but
far from the millions that Netflix had. This undoubtedly simplified its
transition and reduced the likelihood of a backlash. More intriguingly,
Glitch/Slack maintained the support of venture capital investors, who
had initially invested in a very different concept.

Microsoft's shift to cloud services offers another example of executing quickly but with humility. Microsoft took pains to contextualize and
justify the shift as consistent with its overarching storyline and ambitions.[17] Among its many outreach efforts to reconcile audiences to the
move was an informative multipart series called "Expedition Cloud: A
once-in-a-generation paradigm shift." (The company has been a virtual
publishing house of content on the transition, including videos, case
studies, e-books, and blogs.) Expedition Cloud documented Microsoft's
journey, situated the shift within its larger narrative, and admitted past
difficulties. It called the challenges "daunting" and acknowledged that
the move to the cloud was a radical departure from its traditional business (using less stark language). The news that Microsoft was abandoning

its shrink-wrapped software business could have unsettled stakeholders, even those who agreed it was necessary, but taking charge of the narrative seemed to work; journalists generally wrote positively about the move.[18] And, ultimately, the pivot seemed less like a repudiation of the past than a natural evolution of the business.

Conclusion: Maintaining a Consistent Course in Times of Change

Throughout history, great leaders have understood that stories and sense-making are especially important during periods of uncertainty. As more industries are upended and as changes in consumer behavior become more frequent, businesses of all sizes will increasingly face a need for strategic reorientation. How leaders explain and justify their organizations' reinventions will play an outsize role in their ability to endure (see table 8.1). Explorer Roald Amundsen recognized this. On hearing that others had beaten him to the North Pole, he decided to change course—literally. It wasn't the route or the destination that mattered, he told his fellow Norwegians. From the beginning, his had been a mission of scientific discovery. And he had stayed true to that aim: Amundsen went on to become a hero, the first person ever to reach the *South* Pole.

Table 8.1
How to project a consistent vision during inevitable adaptation

Instead of doing this . . .	Do this . . .	And get this result . . .
Launching with a detailed pitch that conveys a well-formed product concept and a precise path to growth and profitability	Craft broad narratives—big-umbrella ambitions that avoid specifying a roadmap in favor of promising to reach a destination.	Room to maneuver, more enthusiasm and support, and ultimately more resources
Reframing each new business iteration with a new goal	Link the new strategic direction to the initial pitch and to your larger aims, especially broad societal missions.	Maintenance of credibility and stakeholder confidence during course corrections; face-saving
Changing course abruptly, and admitting that you were wrong to do so only when stakeholders react negatively	Express empathy and regret when proactively informing people about changes they may not welcome.	Customers and other stakeholders who don't feel abandoned after a major reboot

Conclusion: From Impossible Trade-Offs to Productive Tensions

In the seventeenth century, scientists thought planets orbited in circles, reflecting a divine order. Then along came Johannes Kepler, a German mathematician and astronomer. Kepler, a religious man, initially also believed that the universe exhibited perfect circular patterns. But this theory didn't match his observations that Mars moved in an oval-shaped orbit. And the most recent science—Copernicus's theory that the Sun occupies the center of the universe and is orbited by the planets—also contained inconsistencies. Kepler's genius was to reconcile the best of what was known with the contradictions, and ultimately to acknowledge that planets move in ellipses, not circles. This elegant solution neatly resolved conflicts over such questions as the Sun's position while paving the way for later breakthroughs such as the theory of gravity.

In modern-day organizations, innovation-seeking leaders face similar tensions. Should they focus on what's known and base their key decisions on extensive data? Or should they trust their mental model of the future and improvise a way forward? Is it better to rely on concrete roadmaps or compelling visions? To emphasize efficiency and risk being rigid or to embrace flexibility and risk being wishy-washy? To seek sustainable advantage or temporary wins? Leading innovation is rife with tensions, any of which can cause leaders to stumble.

Even extraordinary leaders of brand-name companies fail to innovate repeatedly and reliably. Failure is often attributed to a lack of money or talent, or bad luck. We think it's something else. Our research has revealed a number of insights, one of which is that leaders struggle to embrace and effectively navigate fundamental tensions inherent in innovation. We've discovered in interactions with hundreds of leaders that the most successful innovators are exceptionally adept at managing such tensions—and that you don't have to be a genius like Kepler to be good at it.

Until now there's been little recognition and exploration of these tensions, and little guidance on how leaders can profitably exploit them. Such omission is problematic because the dynamic environments that most leaders face—contexts characterized by uncertainty, resource scarcity, and high velocity—are highly conducive to tensions.[1] This book has spotlighted these built-in tensions. Each chapter has addressed a fundamental tension—a persistent contradiction, opposition, or puzzle—that consumes leaders' time and attention and requires solution. How do you excite customers about novel products they've never imagined? How can you maintain stakeholders' trust, and keep supporters on board, during a major course correction? Many leaders see such tensions as painful but obligatory trade-offs, and thus reluctantly choose between two narrowly conceived paths. By contrast, we offer an effective new model for leading innovation, one that encourages leaders to see tensions as useful.

The preceding chapters have illustrated the frustration, confusion, and failure that can result when leaders approach tensions rigidly, anticipating forced choices. We have shown how to make tensions more productive—something that can help and be harnessed as leaders seek new opportunities for growth and innovation.

The model we offer simplifies challenges associated with creating new products, services, businesses, and markets. Our message isn't to work harder; the leaders we have met are already exceptionally hard-working. It's to work smarter by addressing innovation's inevitable tensions in the right way: by anticipating the tensions that will arise and facing them head-on, thus reducing the risk of having to halt innovation efforts and better positioning the organization to overcome complications.

How to Tackle Tensions

Whether tensions ultimately harm or fortify an organization depends on how they're addressed, and thus, in many instances, whether they're anticipated. To underline the primacy of *how*, here's a quick review of how to tackle the eight fundamental tensions (also see figure C.1):

1. *Selection versus execution:* Opportunity capture is a two-phase process consisting of opportunity selection and opportunity execution. Shifting from an intense focus during selection to flexibility during execution promotes learning and provides maximum leeway for leaders to adjust adeptly to unforeseen realities.

2. *Differentiation versus borrowing:* In preference to differentiating a new-market business right away, leaders should first engage in "parallel play," taking time to observe what others in the arena are doing, borrowing ideas, and testing them, before fully committing to a business model. Then, again pause, watch, and wait. As the market settles and relationships between actions and outcomes crystallize, update and refine your model.

3. *Accept versus ignore:* We live in an age of data analytics. But stunning advances typically begin with a big beautiful theory or transformative paradigm for which supportive data do not yet exist. In the meantime, leaders should create a virtual barrier within the organization between the data used (or ignored) in the innovation process and the data used in everyday business operations.

4. *Inside versus outside:* To combat cognitive bias and construct a complete picture, leaders should leverage the expertise of dissimilar crowds, both internal and external to the organization. Drawing on the right crowds at the right times, a process known as crowd sequencing, helps accelerate innovation amid uncertainty. Leaders should solicit time-compressed feedback from diverse unorganized groups, then over-deliver for a small "love group," then leverage weak-tie relationships.

5. *Efficiency versus flexibility:* Organizations tend to accumulate policies, routines, and playbooks over time. These fruits of experience improve

Selection vs. Execution

HOW CAN WE CAPTURE NEW GROWTH OPPORTUNITIES MOST EFFECTIVELY?

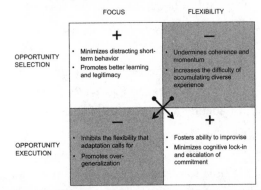

Differentiation vs. Borrowing

HOW DO WE KNOW WHICH POINTS OF DIFFERENTIATION WILL BE MOST IMPORTANT TO WOULD-BE CUSTOMERS?

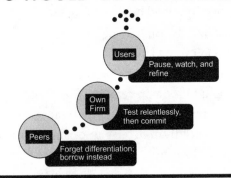

Figure C.1

Accept vs. Ignore

WHEN SHOULD WE DEFER TO THE DATA AND WHEN SHOULD WE IGNORE DATA?

NO   YES

Ignore Data

- When you want to meet the needs of your best (existing) customers

- When you want to overcome common financial hurdles for accepting projects (ROE, ROA, IRR, Payback)

- When you want to introduce a new-to-the-world product category and go after customers who aren't being served at all

- When disruption is afoot and your organization hopes to stave it off

Inside vs. Outside

HOW CAN WE BEST LEVERAGE THE KNOWLEDGE OF OTHERS INSIDE AND OUTSIDE THE ORGANIZATION?

1. PROBLEM UNCERTAINTY

- ❖ Who: An unfocused array of people
- ❖ How: Compress feedback

2. DEMAND UNCERTAINTY

- ❖ Who: A love group
- ❖ How: Overdeliver for extreme users and do things that don't scale up

3. SUPPLY UNCERTAINTY

- ❖ Who: Weak ties
- ❖ How: Create interventions to increase diversity in personal networks

Figure C.1 (continued)

Efficiency vs. Flexibility

HOW CAN WE BUILD OFF THE PAST BUT STILL ADJUST IN THE PRESENT?

Beginning heuristics

Selection • What to do

Procedure • How to do it

Priority • What to do first

Timing • When to transition

Fewer heuristics

More heuristics

Time

Familiar vs. Novel

HOW DO WE FRAME INNOVATIONS IN WAYS THAT GARNER RESOURCES, ATTENTION, AND TRACTION?

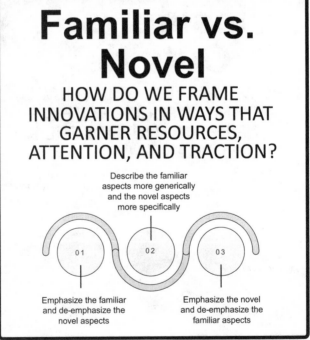

Describe the familiar aspects more generically and the novel aspects more specifically

01   02   03

Emphasize the familiar and de-emphasize the novel aspects

Emphasize the novel and de-emphasize the familiar aspects

Figure C.1 (continued)

Product vs. Purpose

HOW WILL WE CREATE A UNIQUE BRAND ADVANTAGE AND SUSTAIN IT OVER TIME?

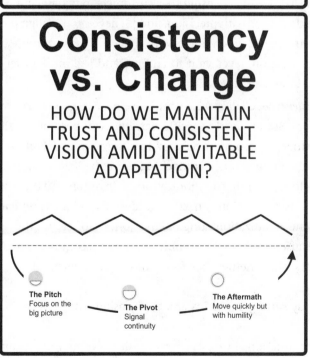

WHAT is the job to be done, that is, the basic problem the customer is facing, and what are the results the customer needs?

WHAT are the experiences in purchasing, using, and living with the product or service we need to provide to solve the problem perfectly?

WHAT processes are needed to provide such experiences?

Consistency vs. Change

HOW DO WE MAINTAIN TRUST AND CONSISTENT VISION AMID INEVITABLE ADAPTATION?

The Pitch
Focus on the big picture

The Pivot
Signal continuity

The Aftermath
Move quickly but with humility

Figure C.1 (continued)

efficiency but can suppress the flexibility that leaders need in dynamic environments. A good way to balance efficiency and flexibility is with heuristics—simple rules of thumb. We have shown that with smart procedures, heuristics can lead to better decisions and rational strategy.

6. *Familiar versus novel:* It's more often customer perception than technological benefit that ultimately determines whether an innovation is adopted. Innovations must appear both familiar and novel to attract attention and gain traction. Our research suggests it's better to emphasize an innovation's similarity to prior solutions—until it takes hold. Once the innovation has gained wider acceptance, an organization should focus on its valuable new attributes.

7. *Product versus purpose:* To create a powerful purpose brand, leaders and innovators should (1) spell out how the product or service addresses a job to be done, that is, how it meets customers' functional, emotional, and social needs; (2) ensure that customers' purchase and use experiences do the job with precision; and (3) develop and align processes to make the brand synonymous with the job. Once a purpose brand has gained traction, leverage it to endorse and legitimize other products that address similar jobs.

8. *Consistency vs. change:* A new initiative needs a good narrative to rally support. But an overly specific narrative can become an albatross if and when it becomes necessary to change course. Early on, leaders should communicate a compelling but inexplicit mission and avoid being too specific in communications to investors and the news media. If a course correction is needed, leaders should focus on consistency with the organization's original mission. It's often not the pivot itself that causes a venture to stumble but how it's communicated to stakeholders, and whether they feel betrayed or understood.

Frequently Arising Scenarios and the Tensions that Govern Them

Different situations bring different tensions to the fore. It can be both grounding and enlightening to recognize, and to anticipate, the shared aspects of a given scenario's characteristic tensions:

1. *An established organization entering a new market.* Leaders entering a new market should maintain operations in existing markets—typically more stable—while fostering change and adapting to a new more dynamic market.

    Typical tensions: In *existing* markets: (1) efficiency versus flexibility, (2) consistency versus change, (3) product versus purpose.

    In *new* markets: (1) familiar versus novel, (2) accept versus ignore, (3) inside versus outside.

2. *A new organization in an established market.* Leaders in this situation should approach the market as both stable and dynamic, quickly developing operational efficiencies to generate necessary economies of scale and in the meantime, treating the market as dynamic, developing an advantageous and unique strategy. By failing to appreciate the environment's stability, a leader may not develop the proficiencies needed to improve reliability; by failing to see the environment as dynamic, a leader may not become adaptable enough to drive differentiation from rivals.

    Typical tensions: (1) selection versus execution, (2) efficiency versus flexibility, (3) differentiation versus borrowing, (4) product versus purpose.

3. *A new organization entering a new market.* In many new markets, leaders of otherwise competing organizations must jointly create basic building blocks, such as norms of exchange and technology standards, that support the functioning of a market.[2] Promoting a new product category in addition to a new product massively increases uncertainty. The risk here is that unforeseen competitors may emerge later and piggyback on such early efforts without sharing their costs (as DJI Technology did to Parrot in consumer drones).[3]

    Typical tensions: (1) familiar versus novel, (2) accept versus ignore (3) inside versus outside, (4) selection versus execution, (5) differentiation versus borrowing.

Tackling Tactics: Prevalent Practices

Ultimately, which tensions leaders address and in what combination matters. The point is to recognize these tensions not as negative but as positive, and embrace them. By embracing the contradictions and incompatibilities, leaders encourage experimentation, which is key to generating novel strategic actions. This leads to an obvious question: Are there common patterns for tackling tensions? We encountered three pathways: sequence, separate, and synthesize.

1. *Sequence.* In certain situations, it makes sense to separate the two poles of a tension in time. If particular forces operate at different times, order matters. This tactic appears relevant for tackling tensions such as familiar versus novel, selection versus execution, and inside versus outside. As one illustration, imagine you are in charge of the introduction of a breakthrough technology that could spawn a new market or a new industry. Emphasizing the familiar features of the new technology will help users feel comfortable enough with the innovation to give it a chance. Later, as the technology takes hold, emphasizing novelty will help ensure that its high-potential attributes aren't overlooked. Sequencing creates continuity between contradictory forces. One (e.g., customers' need for familiarity) paves the way for the other (e.g., introduction of novelty). Thus effective leadership isn't just a matter of juggling tensions, it's also about working out what to do when, and how.

2. *Separate.* A second tactic is to separate the two poles of a single tension. This appears to be relevant for tensions such as differentiation versus borrowing or accepting versus ignoring data. For example, imagine that your data tell you to ignore a new product; it conflicts with your strategy of improving your existing products to better meet the needs of your best customers. You decide to ignore the data and introduce the novel product, despite projected financial returns below those of your mainstream business. In this instance, the leader recognizes that the tension's contradictory forces can inform and benefit one another, and so seeks to exploit both—that is, to rely on data for

current categories and customers but ignore data to go after customers who aren't being served at all.[4] One way to separate the opposing pressures in such a scenario is to create an actual barrier: isolating a small freestanding unit focused solely on the new-to-the-world product from the more profitable mainstream business. Separation allows for a both/and approach to innovation by safeguarding the independence of both groups and their distinctive approaches.[5]

3. *Synthesize.* Sometimes the contradiction between the two poles of a tension can be resolved with a single solution. Consider the tension between efficiency and flexibility. Imagine you lead a technology-based venture tasked with building business in new geographic markets. Adhering to the heuristic "Hire talented locals" will equip your team with an overarching approach to hiring but doesn't prescribe how to do so. The resulting leeway can generate both efficiencies in hiring and local autonomy to improvise hiring specifics in keeping with prevailing circumstances in each country. In one country, your team may turn to a seasoned board of directors to find promising local hires; in another, you might rely on online resources; in a third country, you might use headhunters. Heuristics are thus a single solution that provides both (synthesizes) efficiency and flexibility. Another example of synthesis is organizing around the job to be done—a single solution that helps leaders combine a product or service with a powerful purpose. Such single solutions are not only better remembered among organizational members, and so more likely to be used, but they also generally require less effort than separation approaches, which require multiple solutions.

Tips for Taking in Tensions

Several leaders have asked us how to position themselves better to recognize tensions and orchestrate appropriate responses. We suggest the following:

1. *Cultivate an expansive view of the playing field and the game.* An expansive view of the strategic playing field, and a deep understanding

of the game, encompasses substitutes, complementors, buyers, and suppliers, not just rivals. Such a perspective also focuses attention on the value of alliances and acquisitions to shape the playing field to one's advantage, not just to gain resources. Therefore, while managing tensions requires single-minded attention to the rules for winning the game, it also calls for steady attentiveness to all types of players in the game.

2. *Arrange to learn in a variety of ways.* Equipping yourself to learn in multiple ways simultaneously—such as by trial-and-error, learning from others, and experimentation—can minimize the often stark trade-off between speed and quality in learning. Experimentation and trial-and-error are time-consuming and resource-intensive, but the knowledge generated tends to be high quality; learning from others is quick and inexpensive and can draw on a broad pool of experience, but the resulting knowledge is often lower quality and based on weak causal inferences, and so less likely to head off mistakes. Thus, reliance on a rich combination of direct and indirect approaches to learning, rather than on a particular fine-tuned approach, will help leaders triangulate input.

3. *Don't tune out team members.* Leaders are busy. They are also unavoidably imperfect, and their shortcomings, biases, and blind spots can mar their own and others' performance. Precisely to offset a leader's personal deficiencies, and to guard against being spread too thin, organizations painstakingly assemble strong teams. An exceptional team is particularly crucial in an organization whose leader lacks substantive decision-making experience. Yet despite leaders' need for their team's advice, many are prone to ignore it. Past research suggests that leaders' profiles and proclivities differ from those of other executives, particularly when it comes to micromanaging. Leaders tend to commit more time, energy, and effort to building their organizations; such intense focus and emotional attachment can sometimes prompt them to believe that they alone can guide the organization and juggle the tensions it faces. Sometimes leaders' drive to retain control pushes them to disregard team members when it comes to making

important strategic decisions. This scenario points to a problematic outcome: that tensions and strategic contradictions are often embodied in the relationship between leaders and their colleagues.

Conclusion

In summary, our research reveals a number of key insights. One is that you don't need to be a brilliant visionary to succeed at innovation. Nor is it just about money or luck or who came first to market. Rather, in today's dynamic and complex environment, success is about tackling tensions. The problem is that leaders generally tackle tensions in the wrong way and inadvertently push their organizations backward (see table C.1 for a summary). It doesn't have to be this way. By recognizing and reconciling persistent inconsistencies the right way, leaders can be like Kepler. They can convert what seem to be impossible trade-offs into productive tensions, blessings instead of curses, that pave the way for successful innovation now and in the future.

Table C.1
Summary of Productive Tensions

Tension	Key questions	Why the tension is critical	Inferior tackling of tension	Superior tackling of tension
Familiar vs. novel	How can we frame innovations to garner resources, attention, and traction?	Human perception—perhaps more than technological benefit—will govern whether new products and services thrive or die.	• Highlighting an innovation's distinctiveness during the earliest stage of adoption. • Continuing to emphasize the familiar as a new technology begins to take hold. • Making descriptions of new innovations more general or specific over time.	• Start by emphasizing an innovation's similarity to prior solutions and minimize discussion of what is novel. • Shift to emphasizing the novel as a new technology begins to take hold.
Accept vs. reject	When should we defer to data, and when should we ignore it?	We live in an age of data. Digital platforms, wireless sensors, apps, and mobile phones all amass quantities of data, whose volume doubles every few years.	• Insisting on market research for a market that does not exist. • Having the same people make decisions about existing business operations and future innovations. • Requiring every decision to be backed by quantitative data. • Deferring to data to better meet the needs of best customers.	• Create a structural barrier between the innovation/creative process and the data used in business operations. • Use multiple perspectives drawn from multiple methods (e.g., logic, intuition, qualitative insight). • Ignore the data and think about how to go after customers who aren't being served at all.
Selection vs. execution	How can we capture new growth opportunities most effectively?	Mature corporations, growing businesses, and new ventures all face concerns about how to select and execute opportunities.	• Selecting opportunities in response to emerging customer demand. • Chasing small opportunities that don't merit the time, big opportunities beyond reach, or middle-sized opportunities that are too competitive	• Realize that opportunities have two phases, opportunity selection and opportunity execution, and that selection impacts execution. • Be more focused and disciplined during opportunity selection. • Be more flexible and adaptable during opportunity execution.

Tension	Question	Description		
Inside vs. outside	How can we leverage the knowledge of others both inside and outside the organization?	Leaders need others' help to drive innovation since their information is incomplete, and what they know is distorted by cognitive bias.	• Soliciting feedback from a focus group. • Going after many users who like your product or service so as to allow rapid scaling up. • Drawing on strong-tie relationships to execute a project.	• Temporally compress feedback from an unfocused group. • Do things that don't scale up. • Overdeliver for a few people who love your product or service and use them as stand-ins for future customers. • Leverage weak ties.
Differentiation vs. borrowing	How can we determine which points of differentiation will be most important to customers?	Brand-new markets are like wormholes in science fiction, where the usual rules of time and space do not apply.	• Focusing on differentiating from competitors early on in new markets. • Hedging bets by employing several business model templates. • Trying to perfect a business model—even one that appears to be working well—too early.	• Borrow ideas from substitutes. • Test alternative business model templates quickly and relentlessly, but then commit to one. • Pause, watch, and refine—leave a business model purposely undetermined.
Efficiency vs. flexibility	How can we build on the past but adjust in the present?	To meet competitive threats and adapt, most organizations tend to add more structure over time that inadvertently makes it harder to change.	• Seeing heuristics as biased and dysfunctional, leading to errors in decision making. • Developing heuristics that are applicable to all organizations or unique to a single organization. • Continuing to add more heuristics as experience accumulates.	• View heuristics as useful to decision-making in dynamic settings. • Develop heuristics that are specific in their details but share a common typology (i.e., selection, procedural, priority, and temporal) with those of other organizations. • Simplify and prune existing heuristics.

(continued)

Table C.1 (continued)

Tension	Key questions	Why the tension is critical	Inferior tackling of tension	Superior tackling of tension
Consistency vs change	How can we maintain trust and project a consistent vision amid inevitable adaptation?	To succeed, ventures must rally others around a good story. But often that story turns out to be wrong, and leaders realize they need to change direction.	• Starting with a specific narrative that conveys a well-formed product concept and a path to growth and profitability. • Reframing each new business iteration with a new goal. • Quickly making changes and only defensively admitting mistakes when stakeholders react.	• Craft broad narratives—umbrella ambitions that don't lay out a roadmap but promise to reach a destination. • Make the link between the new strategic direction and the initial pitch obvious and explicitly align it with larger aims. • Use empathy and remorse when proactively informing people of changes they may not welcome.
Product vs purpose	How can we create a unique brand advantage and sustain it over time?	Well-designed "purpose brands" can sell themselves, enable premium pricing, and lock out competitors. But far more new brands fail than succeed.	• Focusing too much on brand identity and image. • Thinking customers make purchasing decisions based on product features. • Spending lots of money advertising, marketing, and buying media. • Extending the original purpose brand to other jobs.	• Think more about the basic problem customers are facing and the solution they crave. • Know what experiences are required to perfectly nail a job. • Design and rethink structures to reliably provide these experiences. • Extend the brand to *new products* that can be hired to do the *same job*.

On Theory and Methodology

Inductive theory building is particularly suitable for exploring complex activities and interactions—such as relational and competitive dynamics, resource allocation, idea generation, opportunity capture, market expansion, and industry formation—in dynamic environments that are poorly understood and about which little theory or published evidence exists.[1]

For each case, we collected data in a way that preserves richness—the detail necessary for building a theory—while minimizing bias. We also sought to triangulate the data by using multiple sources and formats.[2] We collected both historical and current data in the form of transcribed interviews, e-mail correspondence, site visits, attendance at industry events, and archival data from websites, blogs, social network profiles, and trade publications.

We then iteratively organized and reorganized the raw data to generate theories linking actions to outcomes. Next, we compared these tentative theories back to the cases, seeking a fit. Specifically, we compared a provisional theory both to a particular case (to determine whether it replicated) and to multiple cases (cross-case analysis). The aim of this process of repeated categorization of data, comparison, and replication was to find a consistent pattern across the cases that in turn yielded a consistently appropriate theory.[3] Each cycle yielded a closer fit of theory with the observed cases. Such a fit may never be perfect, but outliers often turn out to be rich fodder for refinement of the theory. This process of refinement in turn yields theories that are parsimonious (as spare and uncluttered as possible), predictive, and logically coherent across contexts.

Notes

Introduction

1. Carmen Nobel, "Why Companies Fail-and How Their Founders Can Bounce Back," *Working Knowledge*, Harvard Business School, March 7, 2011, https://hbswk .hbs.edu/item/why-companies-failand-how-their-founders-can-bounce-back.

2. Matthew S. Olsen, Derek van Bever, and Seth Verry, "When Growth Stalls," *Harvard Business Review*, June 8, 2008, https://hbr.org/2008/03/when-growth-stalls.

3. Joan Schneider and Julie Hall, "Why Most Product Launches Fail," *Harvard Business Review* August 1, 2014, https://hbr.org/2011/04/why-most-product-launches -fail.

4. For more on how companies change too late, too early, too much, or too little in response to change, and thus end up worse off than if they had done nothing at all, see Christopher B. Bingham and Kathleen M. Eisenhardt, "Position, Leverage and Opportunity: A Typology of Strategic Logics Linking Resources with Competitive Advantage," *Managerial and Decision Economics* 29, no. 2–3 (2008): 241–256, https://doi.org/10.1002/mde.1386; Kathleen M. Eisenhardt, Nathan R. Furr, and Christopher B. Bingham, "CROSSROADS—Microfoundations of Performance: Balancing Efficiency and Flexibility in Dynamic Environments," *Organization Science* 21, no. 6 (2010): 1263–1273, https://doi.org/10.1287/orsc.1100 .0564.

5. For a more comprehensive treatment of the drivers of high-potential startup failure, we recommend Tom Eisenmann, *Why Startups Fail: A New Roadmap for Entrepreneurial Success* (New York: Crown Currency, 2021). See also Amy Whyte, "The 'Problematic,' VC-Threatening Study That Has Split Harvard Professors," *Institutional Investor*, November 12, 2020, https://www.institutionalinvestor.com

/article/b1p6kjmh25s24b/The-Problematic-VC-Threatening-Study-That-Has
-Split-Harvard-Professors.

6. Damon Brown, "Why Elon Musk's Entrepreneurial Failures Should Give You Confidence and Hope," infographic, Inc.com, June 29, 2018, https://www.inc .com/damon-brown/why-elon-musks-entrepreneurial-failures-should-give-you -confidence-hope-infographic.html.

7. Ted Baker and Reed E. Nelson, "Creating Something from Nothing: Resource Construction through Entrepreneurial Bricolage," *Administrative Science Quarterly* 50, no. 3 (2005): 329–366, https://doi.org/10.2189/asqu.2005.50.3.329; Geoffrey Desa and Sandip Basu, "Optimization or Bricolage? Overcoming Resource Constraints in Global Social Entrepreneurship," *Strategic Entrepreneurship Journal* 7, no. 1 (2013): 26–49, https://doi.org/10.1002/sej.1150; Julienne Senyard et al., "Bricolage as a Path to Innovativeness for Resource-Constrained New Firms," *Journal of Product Innovation Management* 31, no. 2 (July 2013): 211–230, https:// doi.org/10.1111/jpim.12091.

8. Annie Duke, *Thinking in Bets: Making Smarter Decisions When You Don't Have All the Facts* (New York: Portfolio/Penguin, 2019).

9. Clayton M. Christensen and Michael E. Raynor, "Why Hard-Nosed Executives Should Care about Management Theory," *Harvard Business Review,* March 2, 2020, https://hbr.org/2003/09/why-hard-nosed-executives-should-care-about-man agement-theory.

10. Thomas W. Lee, *Using Qualitative Methods in Organizational Research* (Thousand Oaks, CA: Sage, 1998); Christopher B. Bingham et al., "Concurrent Learning: How Firms Develop Multiple Dynamic Capabilities in Parallel," *Strategic Management Journal* 36, no. 12 (August 2015): 1802–1825, https://doi.org/10.1002 /smj.2347.

11. Rory McDonald, Emilie Billaud, and Vincent Dessain, "Parrot: Navigating the Nascent Drone Industry," Harvard Business School Case 619-085 (June 2019, rev. September 2019); Henri Seydoux, "Three Lessons from Parrot's Saga," Paris Innovation Review, September 28, 2016, http://parisinnovationreview.com /articles-en/three-lessons-from-parrots-saga.

12. McDonald, Billaud, and Dessain, "Parrot."

13. This example is drawn from Rory McDonald, Clayton M. Christensen, Daniel West, and Jonathan E. Palmer, "Under Armour," Harvard Business School Case 618-020 (January 2018).

14. Kelefa Sanneh, "Skin in the Game," *New Yorker*, March 27, 2014, https://www.newyorker.com/magazine/2014/03/24/skin-in-the-game.

15. Sanneh, "Skin in the Game."

16. Sanneh, "Skin in the Game."

Chapter 1

1. Gabriel Szulanski and Robert J. Jensen, "Presumptive Adaptation and the Effectiveness of Knowledge Transfer," *Strategic Management Journal* 27 (2006): 937–957.

2. Eric Ries, *The Lean Startup: How Today's Entrepreneurs Use Continuous Innovation to Create Radically Successful Businesses* (New York: Crown Business, 2011).

3. Shona L. Brown and Kathleen M. Eisenhardt, "The Art of Continuous Change: Linking Complexity Theory and Time-Paced Evolution in Relentlessly Shifting Organizations," *Administrative Science Quarterly* 42 (1997): 1–34; Amar V. Bhide, *The Origin and Evolution of New Businesses* (New York: Oxford University Press, 2000).

4. Christopher B. Bingham, "Oscillating Improvisation: How Entrepreneurial Firms Create Success in Foreign Market Entries over Time," *Strategic Entrepreneurship Journal*, 3, no. 4 (2009): 321–345.

5. Christopher B. Bingham, Kathleen M. Eisenhardt, and Nathan R. Furr, "What Makes a Process a Capability? Heuristics, Strategy, and Effective Capture of Opportunities," *Strategic Entrepreneurship Journal* 1, nos. 1–2 (2007): 27–47; Christopher B. Bingham and Kathleen M. Eisenhardt, "Rational Heuristics: The 'Simple Rules' That Strategists Learn from Their Process Experiences," *Strategic Management Journal* 32, no.13 (2011): 1437–1464.

6. To understand how organizations capture opportunities in different markets, we conducted more than 150 in-depth interviews with executives at thirty companies on three continents (North America, Asia, and Europe). The interviews lasted forty-five to ninety minutes and were both open- and closed-ended. Interviewees included lower-level managers as well as top-management team members (CEOs, board chairs, executive vice presidents, and business-unit leaders). We also studied organizations at different stages of opportunity capture, including nascent businesses, young companies seeking to expand, and established companies pursuing new growth. We reviewed relevant research in the fields of strategic management and entrepreneurship published in leading academic and practitioner journals over the last twenty years.

7. Kathleen M. Eisenhardt, "Making Fast Strategic Decisions in High-Velocity Environments," *Academy of Management Journal* 32, no. 3 (1989): 543–576; Bhide, *The Origin and Evolution of New Businesses.*

8. K. E. Weick, "The Collapse of Sensemaking in Organizations: The Mann Gulch Disaster," *Administrative Science Quarterly* 38 (1993): 628-652; K. Weick, *Sensemaking in Organizations* (London: Sage, 1995).

9. Claude M. Steele, "The Psychology of Self-Affirmation: Sustaining the Integrity of the Self," in *Advances in Experimental Social Psychology*, vol. 21, ed. L. Berkowitz (New York: Academic Press, 1988), 261–302.

10. Jake Burton Carpenter, "Jake Burton Carpenter, the King of Snowboards," Inc .com, February 14, 2014, https://www.inc.com/magazine201403/liz-welch/burton -snowboards-success-story-.html.

11. Biz Carson, "The Inside Story of How Uber Tried and Failed to Build a FedEx Rival—and Its $69 Billion Valuation Could Be Jeopardized," *Business Insider*, July 8, 2017, https://www.businessinsider.com/insider-uberrush-2017-6. For more on UberRush, see also https://www.businessinsider.com/insider-uberrush-2017-6; https://www.businessinsider.com/insider-uberrush-2017-6.

12. Christopher B. Bingham and Jason P. Davis, "Learning Sequences: Their Existence, Evolution and Effect," *Academy of Management Journal* 55, no. 3 (2012): 611–641.

13. Thomas R. Eisenmann, Michael Pao, and Lauren Barley, "Dropbox: 'It Just Works,'" Harvard Business School Case 811-065 (January 2011, rev. October 2014), https://hbsp.harvard.edu/product/811065-PDF-ENG.

Chapter 2

1. For more on the research and some of the sectors mentioned in this chapter, see Cheng Gao and Rory McDonald, "Shaping Nascent Industries: Innovation Strategy and Regulatory Uncertainty in Personal Genomics," Harvard Business School Working Paper No. 20-095, March 2020 (personal genomics); Rory McDonald, David Lane, and Mel Martin, "Apple Bets on Augmented Reality," Harvard Business School Case 621-007 (September 2020) (augmented reality); and Rory McDonald, Samir Junnarkar, and David Lane, "Marcus by Goldman Sachs," Harvard Business School Case 620-005 (November 2019, rev. December 2019).

2. Michael E. Porter, "What Is Strategy?," *Harvard Business Review* 74, no. 6 (November–December 1996): 78.

3. For more on the concept of parallel play as an approach to innovation, see Rory McDonald and Kathleen Eisenhardt, "Parallel Play: Startups, Nascent Markets, and the Effective Design of a Business Model," *Administrative Science Quarterly* 65, no. 2 (June 2020): 483–523. Portions of this chapter appeared in Rory McDonald and Kathleen Eisenhardt, "The New-Market Conundrum," *Harvard Business Review* 98, no. 3 (May–June 2020): 75–83.

4. Sunil Paul, "The Untold Story of Ridesharing—Part III: The Birth of Sidecar and Ridesharing," March 27, 2017, https://sunilpaul.medium.com/the -untold-story-of-ridesharing-part-iii-the-birth-of-sidecar-and-ridesharing -9f6e6c706d8d.

5. Will Oremus, "Google's Big Break," Slate, October 13, 2013, https://slate .com/business/2013/10/googles-big-break-how-bill-gross-goto-com-inspired -the-adwords-business-model.html.

6. For an excellent introduction to the topic of experimentation in the innovation process, see Stephan Thomke, *Experimentation Works: The Surprising Power of Business Experiments* (Boston: Harvard Business Review Press, 2020). Also see Michael Luca and Max Bazerman, *The Power of Experiments: Decision-making in a Data Driven World* (Cambridge, MA: MIT Press, 2020).

7. Megan Garber, "Instagram Was First Called 'Burbn'," *Atlantic*, July 2, 2014, https://www.theatlantic.com/technology/archive/2014/07/instagram-used-to -be-called-brbn/373815.

8. Mike Maples Jr, "How Instagram Delighted 1 Billion Users . . . But Almost Didn't," *Starting Greatness* (podcast), Floodgate, January 13, 2020, https://greatness .floodgate.com/episodes/how-instagram-delighted-1-billion-usersbut-almost-didnt -8HtnlPfU.

9. Erin Griffith, "A Unicorn Lost in the Valley, Evernote Blows Up the 'Fail Fast' Gospel," *New York Times*, June 28, 2019, https://www.nytimes.com/2019 /06/28/business/evernote-what-happened.html.

10. Ilan Mochari, "The Inside Story of How PayPal Ousted an Early Rival," *Inc.*, July 7, 2014, https://www.inc.com/ilan-mochari/reid-hoffman-excerpt.html.

11. Steve Bodow, "The Money Shot," *Wired*, September 1, 2001, https://www .wired.com/2001/09/paypal.

12. Steve Blank, "Why the Lean Start-Up Changes Everything," *Harvard Business Review* 91, no. 5 (May 2013): 63–72, https://hbr.org/2013/05/why-the-lean -start-up-changes-everything.

13. See Vineet Kumar, "Making 'Freemium' Work: Many Start-ups Fail to Recognize the Challenges of This Popular Business Model," *Harvard Business Review* 92, no. 5 (May 2014): 27–29, https://hbsp.harvard.edu/product/F1405A-PDF -ENG?Ntt=making+freeium+work&itemFindingMethod=Search; and Thomas R. Eisenmann, Michael Pao, and Lauren Barley, "Dropbox: 'It Just Works,'" Harvard Business School Case 811-065 (January 2011, rev. October 2014), https:// hbsp.harvard.edu/product/811065-PDF-ENG.

14. Dropbox, Inc., Form S-1, EDGAR, Securities and Exchange Commission, February 23, 2018, https://www.sec.gov/Archives/edgar/data/1467623/00011931 2518055809/d451946ds1.htm.

15. Clayton Christensen and Jeremy Dann, "SonoSite: A View Inside," Harvard Business School Case 602-056 (August 2001, rev. January 2015), https://hbsp.harvard .edu/product/602056-PDF-ENG?Ntt=sonosite&itemFindingMethod=Search.

16. Kevin Gibbon, "I Can't Wait for You to See What We Do Next," LinkedIn, March 27, 2018, https://www.linkedin.com/pulse/i-cant-wait-you-see-what-we -do-next-kevin-gibbon.

17. Thomas R. Eisenmann and Laura Winig, "Rent the Runway," Harvard Business School Case 812-077 (November 2011, rev. December 2012), https://www .hbs.edu/faculty/Pages/item.aspx?num=41142.

18. Recode Staff, "Full Transcript: Jennifer Hyman, CEO of Rent the Runway, Is Creating the Spotify of Women's Clothes," Vox, February 9, 2017, https://www .vox.com/2017/2/9/14566938/full-transcript-jennifer-hyman-ceo-rent-the-runway -subscription-womens-clothes; Alexandra Schwartz, "Rent the Runway Wants to Lend You Your Look," *New Yorker*, October 22, 2018, https://www.newyorker.com /magazine/2018/10/22/rent-the-runway-wants-to-lend-you-your-look.

19. Stefan Thomke and Eric von Hippel, "Customers as Innovators: A New Way to Create Value," *Harvard Business Review*, August 1, 2014, https://hbr.org /2002/04/customers-as-innovators-a-new-way-to-create-value.

Chapter 3

1. Neil Patel, "How Netflix Uses Analytics to Select Movies, Create Content, and Make Multimillion Dollar Decisions," https://neilpatel.com/blog/how-netflix-uses -analytics.

2. Alexis Madrigal, "How Netflix Reverse-Engineered Hollywood," *Atlantic*, January 2 2014, https://www.theatlantic.com/technology/archive/2014/01/how -netflix-reverse-engineered-hollywood/282679.

3. Josef Adalian, "Inside Netflix's TV-Swallowing, Market-Dominating Binge Factory," Vulture, June 11, 2018, https://www.vulture.com/2018/06/how-netflix -swallowed-tv-industry.html.

4. Nicolaus Henke, Jacques Bughin, Michael Chui, et al., "The Age of Analytics: Competing in a Data-Driven World," McKinsey Global Institute, December 7, 2016, https://www.mckinsey.com/business-functions/mckinsey-analytics/our -insights/the-age-of-analytics-competing-in-a-data-driven-world#.

5. Clayton M. Christensen, Karen Dillon, Taddy Hall, and David S. Duncan, *Competing against Luck: The Story of Innovation and Customer Choice* (New York: Harper Business, 2016).

6. Josef Adalian, "Inside the Binge Factory," Vulture, June 2018, https://www .vulture.com/2018/06/how-netflix-swallowed-tv-industry.html.

7. Eric Leifer, "Denying the Data: Learning from the Accomplished Sciences," *Sociological Forum* 7, no. 2 (1992), https://www.jstor.org/stable/684311?seq=1.

8. William Broad and Nicholas Wade, *Betrayers of the Truth* (New York: Simon & Schuster, 1982).

9. Thomas S. Kuhn, *The Structure of Scientific Revolutions*, 2nd ed. (Chicago: University of Chicago Press, 1970).

10. Steve Jobs in an interview with *Business Week*, May 25, 1998.

11. This example was elaborated in Peter Bearman, "Robin Williams and the Long Twentieth Century of American Sociology . . . or Back to the Future," *Sociological Forum* 23, no. 2 (2008): 390–396, https://onlinelibrary.wiley.com /doi/abs/10.1111/j.1573-7861.2008.00069.

12. Eric Leifer, "Denying the Data: Learning from the Accomplished Sciences," *Sociological Forum* 7, no. 2 (1992), https://www.jstor.org/stable/684311 ?seq=1.

13. Viktor Mayer-Schönberger and Kenneth Cukier, *Big Data: A Revolution That Will Transform How We Live, Work, and Think* (New York: Houghton Mifflin Harcourt, 2013).

14. Clayton Christensen has written about this phenomenon. See Clayton M. Christensen, James Allworth, and Karen Dillon, *How Will You Measure Your Life?* (London: Thorsons, 2019).

15. As this example suggests, it's not always a problem with the *data* per se; sometimes it's a matter of how leaders *interact* with the data.

16. Rich Karlgaard, "Big Data's Promise: Messy, Like Us," *Forbes*, July 24, 2013, https://www.forbes.com/sites/richkarlgaard/2013/07/24/big-datas-promise -messy-like-us/?sh=167478d73538.

17. Henri Seydoux, "Three Lessons from Parrot's Saga," Paris Innovation Review, September 28, 2016, http://parisinnovationreview.com/articles-en/three-lessons -from-parrots-saga; Mike Murphy, "This French Drone Company Innovates by Knowing When to Ignore What Consumers Want," Quartz, September 11, 2016, https://qz.com/753538/how-parrot-the-french-drone-company-comes-up-with -new-products.

18. This information was derived from a case on Parrot. See Rory McDonald, Emilie Billaud, and Vincent Dessain, "Parrot: Navigating the Nascent Drone Industry," Harvard Business School Case 619-085 (June 2019, rev. September 2019), https://www.hbs.edu/faculty/Pages/item.aspx?num=58480.

19. For an overview of disruption, we recommend Clayton M. Christensen, Michael E. Raynor, and Rory McDonald, "What Is Disruptive Innovation?," *Harvard Business Review,* December 1, 2015, https://hbr.org/2015/12/what-is -disruptive-innovation; and Clayton M. Christensen et al., "Disruptive Inno-vation: An Intellectual History and Directions for Future Research," *Journal of Management Studies* 55, no. 7 (2018): 1043–1078, https://doi.org/10.1111/joms .12349. For a prescriptive perspective on how established firms can *avoid* disrup-tion in changing times, we recommend Charles A. O'Reilly III and Michael L. Tushman, *Lead and Disrupt: How to Solve the Innovator's Dilemma* (Stanford, CA: Stanford Business Books, 2016).

20. This example is drawn from Clayton M. Christensen, *The Innovator's Dilemma: When New Technologies Cause Great Firms to Fail* (Boston: Harvard Business Review Press, 2016).

21. Quote from Josef Adalian, "Inside the Binge Factory," Vulture, June 2018, https://www.vulture.com/2018/06/how-netflix-swallowed-tv-industry.html.

22. Interview with senior company executive.

Chapter 4

1. Katie Kindelan, "Family Says 'Thank You' to the 'Angels' Who Formed Human Chain to Rescue Them off Florida Coast," *ABC News,* July 17, 2017, https:// abcnews.go.com/US/family-angels-formed-human-chain-rescue-off-florida/story ?id=48676832.

2. H. A. Simon, "A Behavioral Model of Rational Choice," *Quarterly Journal of Economics* (1955): 99–118; J. G. March and H. A. Simon, "Organizations," American Psychological Association, 1958, http://psycnet.apa.org/psycinfo/1958-15040 -000; Amos Tversky and Daniel Kahneman, "Judgment under Uncertainty: Heuristics and Biases," *Science* 185, no. 4157 (1974): 1124–1131; C. Camerer and D. Lovallo, "Overconfidence and Excess Entry: An Experimental Approach," *American Economic Review* 89 (1999): 306–318; J. P. Eggers and L. Song, "Dealing with Failure: Serial Entrepreneurs and the Costs of Changing Industries between Ventures," *Academy of Management Journal* 58 (2015): 1785–1803; B. L. Hallen and E. C. Pahnke, "When Do Entrepreneurs Accurately Evaluate Venture Capital Firms' Track Records? A Bounded Rationality Perspective," *Academy of Management Journal* (2016).

3. H. A. Simon, "Applying Information Technology to Organization Design," *Public Administration Review* 33 (1973): 268–278; Z. Lin and K. M. Carley, "Organizational Response: The Cost Performance Tradeoff," *Management Science* 43 (1997): 217–234.

4. Susan T. Fiske and Shelley E. Taylor, *Social Cognition*, 2nd ed. (New York: McGraw-Hill, 1991); Simon, "A Behavioral Model of Rational Choice."

5. Eric Ries, *The Lean Startup: How Today's Entrepreneurs Use Continuous Innovation to Create Radically Successful Businesses* (New York: Crown Business, 2011).

6. Giovanni Gavetti and Jan W. Rivkin, "On the Origin of Strategy: Action and Cognition over Time," *Organization Science* 18 (2007): 420–439.

7. For further discussion of these and other trade-offs, see Susan L. Cohen, Christopher Bingham, and Benjamin L. Hallen, "Why Are Some Accelerators More Effective? Bounded Rationality and Venture Development," *Administrative Science Quarterly* 64, no. 4 (2019): 810–854.

8. Cohen, Bingham, and Hallen, "Why Are Some Accelerators More Effective?," 828.

9. For more on the cultural benefits of inviting feedback, particularly in innovation contexts, we recommend Amy Edmondson, *The Fearless Organization: Creating Psychological Safety in the Workplace for Learning, Innovation, and Growth* (Hoboken, NJ: John Wiley & Sons, 2018). For more on leading by empowering individuals, we recommend Frances Frei and Anne Morris, *Unleashed: The Unapologetic Leader's Guide to Empowering Everyone around You* (Boston: Harvard Business Review Press, 2020).

10. Tversky and Kahneman, "Judgment under Uncertainty"; Fiske and Taylor, *Social Cognition*; Robert B. Cialdini, *Influence: The Psychology of Persuasion*, rev. ed. (New York: Morrow, 1993); Hayagreeva Rao, Henrich R. Greve, and Gerald F. Davis, "Fool's Gold: Social Proof in the Initiation and Discontinuation of Coverage by Wall Street Analysts," *Administrative Science Quarterly* 46, no. 3 (2001): 502–526.

11. R. K. Yin, *Case Study Research: Design and Methods*, 2nd ed. (Thousand Oaks, CA: Sage, 1994).

12. ExperiencePoint, "Why Extreme Users Are an Innovator's Best Friends," Medium.com, September 29, 2020, https://medium.com/@ExperiencePoint/why -extreme-users-are-an-innovators-best-friends-8a74c2cc51f9.

13. "Alexander Graham Bell," PBS, 1999, https://www.pbs.org/transistor/album1 /addlbios/bellag.html.

14. Michael Blanding, "Pay Attention to Your 'Extreme Consumers," Harvard Business School, July14, 2014, https://hbswk.hbs.edu/item/pay-attention-to -your-extreme-consumers.

15. M. Granovetter, "The Strength of Weak Ties," *American Journal of Sociology* 78, no. 6 (May 1973):1360–1380.

16. M. T. Hansen, "The Search-Transfer Problem: The Role of Weak Ties in Sharing Knowledge across Organization Subunits," *Administrative Science Quarterly* 44, no. 1 (1999): 82–111.

17. Christopher B. Bingham and Jason P. Davis, "Learning Sequences: Their Existence, Evolution and Effect," *Academy of Management Journal* 55, no. 3 (2012): 611–641.

18. For more information about how learning can ensue from enlarging the number and variety of people from whom a leader seeks input see the following: Linda Argote, *Organizational Learning: Creating, Retaining and Transferring Knowledge* (Norwell, MA: Kluwer Academic Publishers, 1999); Melissa A. Schilling, Patricia Vidal, Robert E. Ployhart, and Alexandre Marangoni, "Learning by Doing Something Else: Variation, Relatedness, and the Learning Curve," *Management Science* 49, no. 1 (2003): 39–56; Linda A. Hill, Greg Brandeau, Emily Truelove, and Kent Lineback, *Collective Genius: The Art and Practice of Leading Innovation* (Boston, MA: Harvard Business Review Press, 2014).

19. Jose Ferreira, Pablo Claver, Pedro Pereira, and Thomaz Sebastião, "Remote Working and the Platform of the Future," Boston Consulting Group, October 2020, https://pulse.microsoft.com/uploads/prod/2020/10/BCG-Remote-Working -and-the-Platform-of-the-Future-Oct-2020.pdf. For a full discussion of the remote

future of work, we recommend Tsedal Neeley, *Remote Work Revolution: Succeeding from Anywhere* (New York: Harper Business, 2021).

Chapter 5

1. Gary Hamel and Michele Zanini, "Yes, You Can Eliminate Bureaucracy," *Harvard Business Review*, October 29, 2018, https://hbr.org/2018/11/the-end-of-bureaucracy.

2. In "Judgment under Uncertainty: Heuristics and Biases" (*Science* 185, no. 4157 [1974]): 1124–1131), Amos Tversky and Daniel Kahneman argue that individuals often deviate from rationality by resorting to universal heuristics that lead to systematic errors (biases).

3. Christopher Bingham and Kathleen Eisenhardt, "Rational Heuristics: The 'Simple Rules' Strategists Learn from Their Process Experiences," *Strategic Management Journal* 32, no. 13 (2011): 1437–1464.

4. For example, Goldstein and Gigerenzer (2002) found that laboratory participants using the "fast-and-frugal" recognition heuristic could outperform German residents on the task of identifying which of a pair of German cities had the larger population.

5. Research shows that information-intensive and analytically complex approaches can be less accurate despite more effort. See T. D. Wilson and J. W. Schooler, "Thinking Too Much: Introspection Can Reduce the Quality of Preferences and Decisions," *Journal of Personality and Social Psychology* 60, no. 2 (1991): 181–192. Information-intensive approaches also tend to "overfit" solutions based on past experience and thus can have weak predictive accuracy. See Gerd Gigerenzer and Henry Brighton, "Homo Heuristicus: Why Biased Minds Make Better Inferences," *Topics in Cognitive Science* 1, no. 1 (2009): 107–143.

6. Victor DeMiguel, Lorenzo Garlappi, and Raman Uppal, "Optimal Versus Naive Diversification: How Inefficient Is the 1/N Strategy?," *Review of Financial Studies* 22, no. 5 (2009):1915–1953.

7. Paul J. Taylor, Craig Bennell, and Brent Snook, "The Bounds of Cognitive Heuristic Performance on the Geographic Profiling Task," *Applied Cognitive Psychology* 23, no. 3 (2009):410–430.

8. T. D. Wilson and J. W. Schooler, "Thinking Too Much: Introspection Can Reduce the Quality of Preferences and Decisions," *Journal of Personality and Social Psychology* 60, no. 2 (1991): 181–192.

9. Daniel Kahneman, *Thinking Fast and Slow* (New York: Farrar, Straus and Giroux, 2011)

10. Kahneman, and Tversky, "Judgment under Uncertainty."

11. Stéphanie Joalland, "7 Rules for Writing Short Films," Sundance, December 6, 2012, https://www.raindance.org/7-rules-for-writing-short-films.

12. Bill Murphy, "Google Says It Still Swears by the 20 Percent Rule to Find Big Ideas, and You Should Totally Copy It," *Inc.*, November 1, 2020, https://www.inc.com/bill-murphy-jr/google-says-it-still-uses-20-percent-rule-you-should-totally-copy-it.html.

13. Christopher B. Bingham and Kathleen M. Eisenhardt, "Rational Heuristics: The 'Simple Rules' Strategists Learn from Their Process Experiences," *Strategic Management Journal* 32, no. 13 (2011): 1437–1464.

14. For more on how simple rules evolve over time, see also Christopher B. Bingham, Travis Howell, and Timothy E. Ott, "Capability Creation: Heuristics as Microfoundations," *Strategic Entrepreneurship Journal* 13, no. 2 (2019): 121–153.

15. P. J. Feltovich, J. J. Prietula, and K. A. Ericsson, "Studies of Expertise from Psychological Perspectives," in *The Cambridge Handbook of Expertise and Expert Performance*, ed. K. A. Ericsson, N. Charness, P. J. Feltovich, and R. R. Hoffman (New York: Cambridge University Press, 2006), 41–68.

16. Neil Charness, Eyal M. Reingold, Marc Pomplun, and Dave M. Strampe, "The Perceptual Aspect of Skilled Performance in Chess: Evidence from Eye Movements," *Memory and Cognition* 29 (2001): 1146–1152; Michelene H. Chi, Paul J. Feltovich, and Robert Glaser, "Categorization and Representation of Physics Problems by Experts and Novices," *Cognitive Science* 5 (1981): 121–152; Ellen J. Langer and Lois G. Imber, "When Practice Makes Imperfect: Debilitating Effects from Overlearning," *Journal of Personality & Social Psychology* 37, no. 11 (1979): 2014–2024.

17. See also Jason P. Davis, Kathleen M. Eisenhardt, and Christopher B. Bingham, "Optimal Structure, Market Dynamism, and the Strategy of Simple Rules," *Administrative Science Quarterly* 54, no. 3 (2009):413–452. This article demonstrates that simple rules are essential in unpredictable markets. The optimal number of heuristics converges on a narrow range where the relationship between the number of heuristics and performance takes the form of an inverted V.

Chapter 6

1. Nir Eyal, "People Don't Want Something Truly New, They Want the Familiar Done Differently . . . ," *Entrepreneur*, June 18, 2015, https://www.entrepreneur.com/article/247467.

2. C. Bingham and S. Kahl, "The Process of schema Emergence: Assimilation, Deconstruction, Unitization and the Plurality of Analogies," *Academy of Management Journal* 56, no. 1 (2013): 14–34.

3. M. Tripsas and G. Gavetti, "Capabilities, Cognition and Inertia: Evidence from Digital Imaging," *Strategic Management Journal* 2, no. 10/11 (2000): 1147–1162; S. Kaplan and M. Tripsas, "Thinking about Technology: Applying a Cognitive Lens to Technical Change." *Research Policy*, 37, no. 5 (2008): 790–805.

4. V. Rindova and A. Petkova, "When Is a New Thing a Good Thing? Technological Change, Product Form Design, and Perceptions of Value for Product Innovations," *Organization Science* 18, no. 2 (2007): 217–232; A. Hargadon and Y. Douglas, "When Innovations Meet Institutions: Edison and the Design of the Electric Light," *Administrative Science Quarterly* 46 (2001): 476–501.

5. M. L. Gick and K. J. Holyoak, "Schema Induction and Analogical Transfer," *Cognitive Psychology* 15, no. 1 (1983): 1–38; C. Bingham and S. Kahl, "The Process of Schema Emergence: Assimilation, Deconstruction, Unitization and the Plurality of Analogies," *Academy of Management Journal* 56, no. 1 (2013): 14–34.

6. For example, see A. Hargadon and A. Fanelli, "Action and Possibility: Reconciling Dual Perspectives of Knowledge in Organizations," *Organization Science*, 13, no. 3 (2002): 290–302.

7. "Why QR Codes Are on the Rise," *Economist,* November 2, 2017, https://www.economist.com/the-economist-explains/2017/11/02/why-qr-codes-are-on-the-rise; David Pierce, "The Curious Comeback of the Dreaded QR Code," *Wired,* July 10, 2017, https://www.wired.com/story/the-curious-comeback-of-the-dreaded-qr-code; Tyler DeVooght, "The Fall and Rise of the QR Code," Business 2 Community, September 4, 2019, https://www.business2community.com/marketing/the-fall-and-rise-of-the-qr-code-02236397.

8. Richard D'Aveni, "The 3-D Printing Playbook." *Harvard Business Review,* November 27, 2019,https://hbr.org/2018/07/the-3-d-printing-playbook.

9. Damon Lavrinc. "Why Flipping through Paper-like Pages Endures in the Digital World," *Wired,* May 2012, https://www.wired.com/2012/05/why-flipping-through-paper-like-pages-endures-in-the-digital-world.

10. M. T. H. Chi, P. J. Feltovich, and R. Glaser, "Categorization and Representation of Physics Problems by Experts and Novices," *Cognitive Science* 5 (1981): 121–152.

11. See C. Bingham and S. Kahl, "The Process of Schema Emergence: Assimilation, Deconstruction, Unitization and the Plurality of Analogies," *Academy of Management Journal* 56, no. 1 (2013): 14–34.

12. Hewlett Packard Enterprise, "What Is Edge Computing? Enterprise IT Definitions," HPE.com, https://www.hpe.com/us/en/what-is/edge-computing.html; Paul Miller, "What Is Edge Computing?," *Circuit Breaker* (blog), The Verge, May 7, 2018, https://www.theverge.com/circuitbreaker/2018/5/7/17327584/edge-computing -cloud-google-microsoft-apple-amazon.

13. Chris Anderson, "Drones Go to Work," *Harvard Business Review*, May 16, 2017, https://hbr.org/2017/05/drones-go-to-work.

Chapter 7

1. Professor Clayton Christensen articulated this simple but powerful insight in 2005, asserting that, thanks to big data and sophisticated analysis tools, business leaders knew more about their customers than ever before, but misunderstood why people make purchases: people don't buy things because they fit a particular demographic or psychographic profile; they "hire" products to make progress in the circumstances in which they find themselves. For more on the concept of jobs to be done, see Theodore Levitt, "Marketing Myopia," *Harvard Business Review* 82, no. 7–8 (July–August 2004): 138–149. https://hbr.org/2004/07/marketing-myopia; C. M. Christensen, T. Hall, K. Dillon, et al., "Know Your Customers' 'Jobs to Be Done,'" *Harvard Business Review* 94, no. 9 (September 2016): 54–62; and Clayton M. Christensen, Taddy Hall, Karen Dillon, and David S. Duncan, *Competing against Luck: The Story of Innovation and Customer Choice* (New York: Harper Business, 2016).

2. Clayton M. Christensen, Rory McDonald, Laura E. Day, and Shaye Roseman, "Integrating around the Job to Be Done," Harvard Business School Module Note 611-004 (2020).

3. The steps in this process are drawn from Christensen et al., "Integrating around the Job to Be Done."

4. Erich Joachimsthaler and David A. Aaker, "Building Brands without Mass Media," *Harvard Business Review* 75 no. 1–2 (January–February 1997): 39–50.

5. This chapter, including the conceptualization of purpose brands, draws on and extends an essay by Harvard Business School professors Rory McDonald and Clayton Christensen and research associate Shaye Roseman. See Rory McDonald, Clayton M. Christensen, and Shaye Roseman, "Purpose Brands," Harvard Business School Module Note 619-075 (June 2019, rev. July 2020), https://www.hbs.edu/faculty/Pages/item.aspx?num=56144.

6. Clayton M. Christensen, Scott Cook, and Taddy Hall, "It's the Purpose Brand, Stupid," *Wall Street Journal*, November 29, 2005.

7. The next two paragraphs draw from GOJO Industries' corporate history. See https://www.gojo.com/en/About-GOJO/History.

8. For readers interested in the origins of such products and their development by large organizations, we recommend Gary P. Pisano, *Creative Construction: The DNA of Sustained Innovation* (New York: PublicAffairs, 2019).

9. Joe Pinsker, "A Drink for Babies Is No Hangover Cure," *Atlantic*, June 3, 2015, https://www.theatlantic.com/health/archive/2015/06/a-drink-for-babies -is-no-hangover-cure/394685.

10. Andria Cheng, "Pedialyte Sales Grow—into an Adult Market," *Wall Street Journal*, May 13, 2015, https://www.wsj.com/articles/pedialyte-sales-growinto -an-adult-market-1431560650.

11. Bailey King, "Pedialyte Finally Launches Product Made for Treating Hangovers," *PhillyVoice*, December 27, 2018, https://www.phillyvoice.com/pedialyte -hangover-cure-sparkling-rush-powder-packs.

12. Kaitlyn Tiffany, "How Pedialyte got Pedialit," Vox, September 10, 2018, https://www.vox.com/the-goods/2018/9/10/17819358/pedialyte-hangover -marketing-strategy-instagram-influencers.

13. This section draws on a Harvard Business School teaching case study. See Rory McDonald, Clayton M. Christensen, Daniel West, and Jonathan E. Palmer, "Under Armour," Harvard Business School Case 618-020 (January 2018).

14. Daniel Roberts, "Maryland Football's Best Corporate Friend," *Fortune*, November 20, 2012, http://fortune.com/2012/11/20/maryland-footballs-best -corporate-friend.

15. Chuck Salter, "Protect This House," *Fast Company*, August 1, 2005.

16. Prophet.com, "'I Will' vs. 'Just Do It.'" https://www.linkedin.com/pulse /20140818213434-2171492--i-will-vs-just-do-it-the-under-armour-success-story.

17. Kevin Plank, interview with author, April 14, 2017.

18. Kevin Plank, "Under Armour's Founder on Learning to Leverage Celebrity Endorsements," *Harvard Business Review*, May 2012; Kevin Plank, interview with author, April 14, 2017.

19. "Under Armour Startup Story," Fundable.com, n.d.

20. "Under Armour Startup Story"; Kelefa Sanneh, "Skin in the Game," *New Yorker*, March 24, 2014, http://www.newyorker.com/magazine/2014/03/24/skin-in-the-game.

21. Sanneh, "Skin in the Game."

22. Sanneh, "Skin in the Game."

23. Callahan, "No Sweat"; Plank, interview, April 14, 2017.

24. Plank, interview, April 14, 2017.

25. Plank, "Under Armour's Founder on Learning to Leverage Celebrity Endorsements."

26. Kip Fulks, interview with author, June 1, 2017.

27. Matthew Philips, "How Under Armour Tackled Nike and Adidas," *Newsweek*, October 14, 2009.

28. Plank, interview, April 14, 2017.

29. Plank, interview, April 14, 2017; Callahan, "No Sweat."

30. Plank, interview, April 14, 2017.

31. "The Donald Dell Interview: Plank Tells Story of Getting UA in *Any Given Sunday*," CSN Mid-Atlantic, July 17, 2016, http://www.csnmidatlantic.com/video/kevin-plank-tells-story-getting-under-armour-any-given-sunday.

32. Plank, "Learning to Leverage Celebrity Endorsements."

33. Plank, interview, April 14, 2017.

34. Chuck Salter, "Protect This House," Fast Company, August 1, 2005.

35. See Al Ries and Jack Trout, *Positioning: The Battle for Your Mind* (New York: McGraw-Hill, 1981); and David Aaker, "Ries & Trout Were Wrong: Brand Extensions Work," *Harvard Business Review*, April 2012.

36. David Aaker, "Brand Extensions: The Good, the Bad, and the Ugly," *MIT Sloan Management Review* 47 (1990): 47.

37. This section was adapted from McDonald et al., "Purpose Brands."

38. This example is drawn from Christensen et al., *Competing against Luck*, 145.

39. Blake Z. Rong, "The Future of Volvo," *Autoweek*, December 29, 2013, https://www.autoweek.com/news/a1947476/future-volvo.

40. This section draws on Clayton M. Christensen and Michael E. Raynor, *The Innovator's Solution* (Boston: Harvard Business Review Press, 2013).

41. Fulks, interview, June 1, 2017.

42. Rina Raphael, "Female Founders Give Scrubs a Functional, Fashionable Make-over," *Fast Company*, July 6, 2018, https://www.fastcompany.com/40589057/female-founders-give-scrubs-a-functional-fashionable-makeover.

43. Dan Neil, "What Part of 'Mini' Did You Not Grasp, BMW?," *Wall Street Journal*, March 5, 2011, https://www.wsj.com/articles/SB100014240527487046 15504576172832123217962.

44. Timothy Cain, "Mini Sales Figures—US Market," Good Car Bad Car, 2021, https://www.goodcarbadcar.net/mini-us-sales-figures.

45. Steph Willems, "QOTD: What to Do with Mini?," May 16, 2017, https://www.thetruthaboutcars.com/2017/05/qotd-what-to-do-with-mini; Matt Posky, "Mini Dealers Want to Know What the Hell Is Going On with the Brand," The Truth about Cars, March 22, 2018, https://www.thetruthaboutcars.com/2018/03/mini-dealers-want-know.

Chapter 8

1. Norwegian Polar Institute, "Did You Know That Amundsen Was Actually Supposed to Go to the North Pole?," October 20, 2011, https://nettarkiv.npolar.no/sorpolen2011.npolar.no/en/did-you-know/2011-10-20-amundsen-was-meant-to-go-to-the-north-pole.html.

2. Portions of this chapter originally appeared in Rory McDonald and Robert Bremner, "When It's Time to Pivot, What's Your Story? How to Sell Stakeholders on a New Strategy," *Harvard Business Review* 98, no. 5 (September–October 2020): 98–105.

3. Amar V. Bhide, *The Origin and Evolution of New Businesses* (Oxford: Oxford University Press, 2003).

4. Thomas Eisenmann, Eric Ries, and Sarah Dillard, "Hypothesis-Driven Entrepreneurship: The Lean Startup," Harvard Business School Background Note 812-095 (December 2011, rev. July 2013), https://www.hbs.edu/faculty/Pages/item.aspx?num=41302.

5. The research that undergirds this chapter was conducted by Professors Rory McDonald (Harvard Business School) and Cheng Gao (University of Michigan).

For more detail on the methodology and data collection, see Rory McDonald and Cheng Gao, "Pivoting Isn't Enough? Managing Strategic Reorientation in New Ventures," *Organization Science* 30, no. 6 (2019): 1289–1318, https://doi.org/10.1287/orsc.2019.1287.

6. See M. Tomz and R. P. Van Houweling, "The Electoral Implications of Candidate Ambiguity," *American Political Science Review* 103, no. 1 (2009): 83–98; and C. R. Grose, N. Malhotra, and R. P. Van Houweling, "Explaining Explanations: How Legislators Explain Their Policy Positions and How Citizens React," *American Journal of Political Science* 59, no. 3 (2016): 724–743.

7. Willy Shih and Stephen Kaufman, "Netflix in 2011," Harvard Business School Case 615-007 (August 2014), https://www.hbs.edu/faculty/Pages/item.aspx?num=47834.

8. Nicolás Rivero, "Magic Leap Tried—and Failed—to Pivot from Delightful Consumer Tech to 'Lethal' Military Gear," Quartz, November 30, 2018, https://qz.com/1481082/magic-leap-tried-to-get-a-contract-to-build-combat-gear-for-the-army.

9. Guy Raz, "Away: Jen Rubio," *How I Built This with Guy Raz*. NPR, March 18, 2019, https://www.npr.org/2019/03/08/701651787/away-jen-rubio.

10. See A. M. Grant and S. Sonnentag, "Doing Good Buffers against Feeling Bad: Prosocial Impact Compensates for Negative Task and Self-Evaluations," *Organizational Behavior and Human Decision Processes* 111, no. 1 (2010): 13–22.

11. Susie Allen, "Hierarchies and Prototypes: Lessons from the Drone and Video Game Industries," *Stanford eCorner*, July 10, 2019, https://ecorner.stanford.edu/articles/hierarchies-and-prototypes-lessons-from-the-drone-and-video-game-industries.

12. "Salesforce Introduces New Einstein Services, Empowering Every Admin and Developer to Build Custom AI for Their Business," Salesforce.com, April 17, 2019, https://www.salesforce.com/news/press-releases/2019/04/17/salesforce-introduces-new-einstein-services-empowering-every-admin-and-developer-to-build-custom-ai-for-their-business. For a broader view of how artificial intelligence is reshaping organizations, we recommend Marco Iansiti and Karim Lakhani, *Competing in the Age of AI: Strategy and Leadership When Algorithms and Networks Run the World* (Boston, MA: Harvard Business Review Press, 2020).

13. Dana Hull, "Tesla Stores Start to Re-open after U-Turn on Retail Strategy," Bloomberg, March 11, 2019, https://www.bloomberg.com/news/articles/2019-03-11/tesla-stores-start-to-re-open-after-u-turn-on-retail-strategy.

14. Shih and Kaufman, "Netflix in 2011."

15. Hiten Shah, "How Slack Became a $16 Billion Business by Making Work Less Boring," *Nira* (blog), https://usefyi.com/slack-history.

16. "A Sad Announcement from Tiny Speck," Glitch, https://web.archive.org/web /20130102151524/http://www.glitch.com/closing.

17. Simon London, "Microsoft's Next Act," *McKinsey Quarterly* (podcast), April 3, 2018, https://www.mckinsey.com/industries/technology-media-and-telecommuni cations/our-insights/microsofts-next-act.

18. Gene Marks, "How Much Will Microsoft's Pivot to the Cloud Boost Quarterly Earnings?" *Fox Business*, July 17, 2018, https://www.foxbusiness.com/small -business/will-microsofts-pivot-to-the-cloud-boost-quarterly-earnings.

Conclusion

1. Kathleen M. Eisenhardt, Nathan R. Furr, and Christopher B. Bingham, "CROSSROADS—Microfoundations of Performance: Balancing Efficiency and Flexibility in Dynamic Environments," *Organization Science* 21, no. 6 (2010): 1263–1273, https://doi.org/10.1287/orsc.1100.0564.

2. Brandon H. Lee, Jeroen Struben, and Christopher B. Bingham, "Collective Action and Market Formation: An Integrative Framework," *Strategic Management Journal* 39, no. 1 (2017): 242–266, https://doi.org/10.1002/smj.2694.

3. For more on these types of problems, see Jeroen Struben, Brandon H. Lee, and Christopher B. Bingham, "Collective Action Problems and Resource Allocation during Market Formation," *Strategy Science* 5, no. 3 (2020): 245–270, https://doi.org/10.1287/stsc.2020.0105.

4. For example, the dual headquarters adopted by Softcorp, a Dutch software company, helped it achieve global integration (in Europe) and local responsiveness (in Asia). See Julian Birkinshaw et al., "How Do Firms Manage Strategic Dualities? A Process Perspective," *Academy of Management Discoveries* 2, no. 1 (2016): 51–78, https://doi.org/10.5465/amd.2014.0123. The paper treats tensions as contradictory forces that require mutually exclusive solutions.

5. For more on how to manage tensions, see some fine work by Wendy Smith and her colleagues: Wendy K. Smith and Marianne W. Lewis, "Toward a Theory of Paradox: A Dynamic Equilibrium Model of Organizing," *Academy of Management Review* 36, no. 2 (January 2011): 381–403, https://doi.org/10.5465/amr.2011

.59330958; Wendy K. Smith and Michael L. Tushman, "Managing Strategic Contradictions: A Top Management Model for Managing Innovation Streams," *Organization Science* 16, no. 5 (2005): 522–536, https://doi.org/10.1287/orsc.1050 .0134; and Wendy K. Smith, "Dynamic Decision Making: A Model of Senior Leaders Managing Strategic Paradoxes," *Academy of Management Journal* 57, no. 6 (2014): 1592–1623, https://doi.org/10.5465/amj.2011.0932.

On Methodology and Theory

1. Kathleen M. Eisenhardt, "What Is the Eisenhardt Method, Really?," *Strategic Organization* 19, no. 1 (2021): 147–160, https://doi.org/10.1177/1476127020982866; Kathleen M. Eisenhardt and Melissa E. Graebner, "Theory Building from Cases: Opportunities and Challenges," *Academy of Management Journal* 50, no. 1 (2007): 25–32, https://doi.org/10.5465/amj.2007.24160888.

2. Eisenhardt, "What Is the Eisenhardt Method, Really?"; Kathleen M. Eisenhardt and Melissa E. Graebner, "Theory Building from Cases: Opportunities And Challenges," *Academy of Management Journal* 50, no. 1 (2007): 25–32, https://doi.org/10 .5465/amj.2007.24160888.

3. Kathleen M. Eisenhardt, "Building Theories from Case Study Research," *Academy of Management Review* 14, no. 4 (1989): 532–550, https://doi.org/10.4135 /9781473915480.n52.

Index

Chevrolet, 52
Chick-Fil-A, 57–58
Christensen, Clayton, 83–85,
  142n1
Clark, Kelly, 12
Clemson University, 90
CME Group, 15
CNBC, 107
Cognitive lock-in, 8–9
Comfort. *See* Familiarity
Commitment, after testing, 25–26
Complexity, 57
Computers, 75–76, 79–80
Consistency, xxii–xxiii, 100,
  103–106
Consumers. *See* Customers
Cook, Frederick, 99
Cook, Scott, 86
Copernicus, Nicolaus, 111
COVID-19, 58, 88, 100
Craigslist, 85
Crest toothpaste, 92
Crowd sequencing, xxi
  benefits of, 47–48, *56*
  defined, 46, 55
  demand uncertainty, 48–53
  focus groups vs., 46–47
  in innovative/uncertain
    environments, xxi, 45–56, *56*,
    113, *115*
  problem uncertainty, 46–48
  supply uncertainty, 53–55
Cruise Automation, 24
Cuban missile crisis, 43
Cukier, Kenneth, 39
Customers
  data on, 33
  in innovative/uncertain
    environments, xx, 20–21, 26, 28

listening and responding to, xxii, 4,
  11, 15, 16, 24, 29, 46–53, 83–85
  opportunistic response to, xx, 4, 10
  product purchase choices, 39,
    83–85, *84*, 142n1

Data
  analytics, 34–35, 37
  decision-making role of, xx–xxi, 34,
    39
  deferring to, xx–xxi, 34–35, 36, 40
  ignoring, xx–xxi, 34, 35–42, *40*
  in innovative/uncertain
    environments, 35, 37–38, 40–44,
    44, 113, *115*
  limitations of, 35–36, 39–42
  scientists' use of, xxi, 35–37
  successful uses of, xx, 33–34
Data barriers, 42–43
Davis, Jason, 140n17
Decision-making
  data's role, xx–xxi, 34–35, 39
  devil's advocate role, 43
  heuristics, xxi, 57–69
  product purchase choices, 39, 83–85,
    84, 142n1
Delivery.com, 13
Demand uncertainty, 48–53
Denso Wave, 76
Diard, Jean-Luc, 12
Dick's Sporting Goods, 13
Diet Coke, 92
Differentiation, xx, 20, 23
Digg, xii
Discipline, in opportunity selection
  and execution, xx, 3–18
Disk drives, 41–42
Disruption, 41–42
DJI Technology, xvii, 41

Heuristics (cont.)
  guidelines, *69*
  organizational, 60–65, *65*, 69, *116*,
    118
  simplification of, 65–69
  uniform structure of, 64, 69
  universal, 60
Hoka One One, 12–13
Holmes, Elizabeth, xii
Honda, xix
Honda, Ridgeline, 51–52
Horowitz, Andreessen, 108
House of Cards (television series), 33
Houston, Drew, 16
Humility, 106–109
Hyman, Jenn, 29

IKEA, 84, 85
Inductive method, xv, 127
Information. *See* Data
Information-intensive approaches,
    139n5
Innovation and innovative
  organizations. *See also* Startups
  borrowing and, 22–29
  change and responsiveness in,
    xxii–xxiii, 99–109, *101*
  crowd sequencing as tool of, 45–46
  data's role, 35, 37–38, 40–44, *44*,
    113, *115*
  differentiation impossible in
    context of, 20–21
  expansion of, 19
  explanations of successful, xii–xiv
  framing/marketing, xvi–xvii, xxii,
    73–82, *82*, *116*, 118
  operating procedures, xxi, 55–69
  parallel play, xx, 21
  protection and nurturing of, 42–44

scientific, xxi, 35–37
  success/failure rate of, xi, 111
  testing and commitment as
    characteristic of, 25–26
In-N-Out Burger, xix, 62
Instagram, xix, 25
Insurance industry, 75, 79
Intercontinental Exchange, 15
Internet of Things (IoT), 80
Intuit, 86–87
iPad, 37
iPhone, 92
iPod, 40
Italian Job, The (film), 96

Joachimsthaler, Erich, 86
Jobs, Steve, xii, 37, 40, 54
JPMorgan Chase, 15

Kahneman, Daniel, 58, 60–61,
    139n2
Kalanick, Travis, 13
Kennedy, John F., 43
Kennedy, Robert, 43
Kepler, Johannes, 111, 123
Kindle, 79
Korey, Steph, 103
Kuhn, Thomas, *The Structure of
  Scientific Revolutions*, 36–37

Leaders and leadership
  in dynamic environments, xi–xiii
  effective, xii, xiv, 19–20, 112
  openness of, to team members,
    122–123
  opportunistic vs. strategic, 4–13
  parallel play of, 21–22, 30
  rules and patterns exhibited by,
    19–20